"In *LORE* Jeanette Schneider dares us to look at our truest selves, encourages us to throw off the chains tying us down, and leads the way for us to become members of fierce female tribes—ones that will hold, protect, and inspire us. Schneider is a force on the page—a mentor, a champion and a loving advocate."

**–Randy Susan Meyers, bestselling author of The Widow of Wall Street**

"Jeanette provides a life manual for the woman who is ready to fly! She instigates deep introspection, self-reflection, and ownership of your past, present, and future self. She provides a framework for admitting, acknowledging, and accepting who you are created to become. Ms. Schneider speaks the language of acceptance, grace, and forgiveness without leaving room for excuses and self-pity, only love. Thank you Jeanette for giving us a spring board into freedom!"

**– Dr. Melanie Ross Mills, Author, Radio Host, Relationship Expert**

"Jeanette allows you to realize it's never too late to change your path and shift the perception of your past to view it as a gift you can apply toward your future."

**–Amy Jo Martin, bestselling author of Renegades Write The Rules**

"Jeanette Schneider has crafted a gorgeous guide for women who are ready to master the most important relationship in their lives - the one with themselves. Fusing wise recommendations, evocative stories, heart-opening writing prompts, and aha-inducing activities, *LORE* is one of those books you'll return to over and over again - and share with all of your girlfriends - because it makes you laugh, it makes you cry, and most importantly, shows you how to reclaim the role of protagonist in your life."

**–Alexia Vernon, Author, Step Into Your Moxie**

"Jeanette's personality and conviction radiate off the page. She is empathizer, vulnerable narrator, mission-focused guide, conscious mom and gender rights badass... all rolled into one."

**– Bill Reishtein, SVP, Group Creative Director, Arc Worldwide**

"In LORE: Harnessing Your Past To Create Your Future, Jeanette Schneider invites her readers to embark on a daring new journey. Like any quest worth the taking, the way is fraught with demons and shape-shifters, hidden pitfalls and the need for constant vigilance. As the old saying goes, I can't promise you it will be easy, but I promise you it'll be worth it. At once humorous, hard-hitting, and encouraging, Jeanette has curated letters and shared the experiences of some fierce and awe-inspiring women (herself included). These serve as models of how to reframe the lore and messaging from family, society, and circumstances into new stories of empowerment, fulfillment, and promise for women today and the next generations. The girl you were and the woman you're becoming are waiting to hear from you, and waiting for you to embrace the miracle of who you are today."

**– Marc Graham, author of the award-winning novel Of Ashes and Dust**

JEANETTE SCHNEIDER

# LORE

*Harnessing Your Past*
*To Create Your Future*

BALBOA
PRESS

A DIVISION OF HAY HOUSE

Balboa Press books may be ordered through booksellers or by contacting:

Balboa Press
A Division of Hay House
1663 Liberty Drive
Bloomington, IN 47403
www.balboapress.com
1 (877) 407-4847

Print information available on the last page.

ISBN: 978-1-9822-0156-2 (sc)
ISBN: 978-1-9822-0154-8 (hc)
ISBN: 978-1-9822-0155-5 (e)

Library of Congress Control Number: 2018903917

Balboa Press rev. date: 06/13/2018

This book is a work of non-fiction. Unless otherwise noted, the author and the publisher make no explicit guarantees as to the accuracy of the information contained in this book and in some cases, names of people and places have been altered to protect their privacy.

# Contents

Introduction ................................................................................ xix

## Part I: The Past—Forgive

1. Uncover Your Messaging ............................................................ 1

   **Do the Work - Reflection Point**

2. Finding Truth—Belief Systems .................................................. 7

   **Do the Work - Belief Systems**

3. You Got It from Your Mama ..................................................... 13

   **Do the Work - Self-Talk**

4. Tragic Life Events ..................................................................... 18

   **Do the Work - Self-Care**

5. Forgiveness ............................................................................... 23

   **Do the Work - The Intention of Forgiveness**

   **Do the Work - Hot Letters**

Part I Key Takeaways ................................................. 33

6. The Letters—Forgiving the Past ............................................. 34
   Chelli Wolford............................................................. 39
   Caroline Heldman........................................................ 43
   Camille DiMaio ........................................................... 48
   Kimberly Derting ......................................................... 53

7. Writing Your Love Letter—Getting Started ........................... 56
   **Do the Work - Visualizing Your Younger Self**
   **Do the Work - Going Deeper**

8. Free-Writing .............................................................. 62

9. Emotional Writer's Block........................................... 64

10. Keep Writing—Keep Going.................................................. 67

**Part II: The Present—Choose**

11. Choose to Choose............................................................ 71
    **Do the Work - Deathbed Wishes**

12. The Gut-Check Method ........................................... 76
    **Do the Work - The Gut Check**

13. Active Orientation ........................................................ 80
    **Do the Work - Active-Choice Orientation**

14. Choice and Self Worth ................................................83

   **Do the Work - Choose Yourself**

15. The Relationships We Choose..................................... 90

   **Do the Work - Reflection Point**

16. Love Yourself First.....................................................95

   **Do the Work - Love Yourself First**

17. Appropriate Boundaries...............................................99

   **Do the Work - Boundaries**

18. Healthy Conflict and Communication ....................................104

   **Do the Work - Healthy Conflict and Intimacy**

19. External Approval and Choice....................................109

   **Do the Work - Perceptions**

20. Overcoming Social Influence.................................... 113

   **Do the Work - Observing Social Influence**

21. Role Modeling........................................................ 118

   **Do the Work - Unfollow, Unfriend, Unload**

22. Your Relationship with Self ..................................... 121

   **Do the Work - Mirror, Mirror**

23. Masculinization vs. Sexualization ............................129

   **Do the Work - The Feminine Spectrum**

Part II Key Takeaways ............................................. 135

24. The Letters—Making Choices................................136
     Jessica Moore....................................................137
     Jamie Little.......................................................141
     Amy Jo Martin ..................................................147
     Sadaf Baghbani ................................................ 153

## Part III: The Future

25. Manifesting ........................................................ 161

**Do the Work - The Wish List**

26. Your Future Self ................................................166

**Do the Work - Visualizing Your Future (or Higher) Self**

     Part III Key Takeaways........................................169

27. The Letters—Manifesting the Future .....................170
     Donna Brazile ..................................................172
     Priya Matthew...................................................178
     Emily Nolan......................................................182

## Part IV: For the Girls

28. Your #girltribe ...................................................190

29. Creating Your Daughter's #girltribe ........................192

**Do the Work - Reflection Point**

30. Conscientious Messaging—

Head, Heart, and Health.........................................196

**Do the Work - Head, Heart, and Health**

31. Mom to Mentor.....................................................201

32. Purposeful Girl Talk............................................205

**Do the Work - Date Night**

**Do the Work - For the Girls: Love Letters to My Future Self**

Part IV Key Takeaways.......................................... 211

33. The Letters—To My Future Self...........................212

Aleena Valdez .....................................................213

34. Conclusion ........................................................ 217

**Part V: Love, Me**

35. The Author's Love Letter to her Younger Self.........221

Acknowledgments.................................................227

Recommended Reading ...........................................229

Dedicated to the memory of
Frieda Wagner Schneider.
Wherever you are, I know you shine.

*If you must look back, do so forgivingly. If you must look forward, do so prayerfully. However, the wisest thing you can do is be present … Gratefully.*

*—Maya Angelou*

*Introduction*

# LORE

*Harnessing Your Past*
*To Create Your Future*

*Lore (noun): a body of traditions and knowledge on a subject or held*
*by a particular group, typically passed person to person by word of mouth.*
*Synonyms: mythology, myths, legends, stories, traditions, folklore, fables,*
*oral tradition, mythos.*
*—Oxford English Dictionary*

S elf-reflection is one of the greatest catalysts for a new way forward. Through it, we discover the essence of how we approach life, how successfully we move from aspiration to actualization, and how we uncover our lore. These are the beliefs we have been immersed in from infancy by those who live alongside us. This book offers you the opportunity to shape your story and write your chapters yourself but only after you are consciously aware of where the story begins.

I have had the honor of having final conversations with those heading on to new adventures. It seems that in the moments between here and there, we are no longer housed in the stories of our lives. The way we've raised our children, our legacies, our prejudices, and our beliefs become inconsequential. It is as if we are able to review our lives in real time, and God, what magic it is if you can be present as someone moves from maligned to wise.

My grandmother, a German immigrant, raised ten children in a three-bedroom home in Florida all the while rocking magenta nail polish and a bite. At the end of her life, we had three incredibly meaningful conversations that will remain with me for the rest of mine. All the family stories about lack, hardship, and our token self-deprecating humor fell away. Our religious biases and deeply entrenched views of ourselves and others were suddenly tagged as nonsense. She asked me to see the world differently, to roll with the big things because they would work themselves out, to pay attention to the little things, and "Love each other every day." Then she asked me if she could leave us.

Many years before, I had a similar conversation with her husband, my grandfather, prior to his decline into Alzheimer's. He raised a brood of children as a devout Jehovah's Witness; in his world, his authority was absolute and the elders reigned supreme. But as we talked about my clashes with faith and my leaders, he shook his head and said, "They are just men, little one. Find your own way." I was stunned that this stoic man, who had breathed the faith of our family, didn't shake his finger at me for my trespasses. Instead, he saw it for what it was as his light began to diminish.

Another man became like a grandfather to me at the end of his life. He had built an incredibly successful business and had achieved a great deal of wealth. He called me the day before he passed to say he was being transferred to hospice care. "Will you come see me?" he asked. I sat next to him as he shooed away my tears with his hands. "Stop crying," he said.

We didn't have time for tears. He had things to tell me. He shared his wishes for me and my daughter and what he needed me to know.

"None of it is important. Money, success, your business. Don't waste your life chasing things. The people who are around your bed when you're dying? Those are the people you should love while you're living."

All of those people, strong in their own right, challenged the messages they'd received throughout their lives and the messaging they instilled in their children and grandchildren. It was as if all the things I knew about them were no longer real, as if they'd never been.

Even with this grand imparted wisdom, I didn't change my life to reflect their wishes for me. No. I got caught up in living—paying bills and handling relationships—and it wasn't until I was responsible for the messaging of another that all this came rushing back wrapped in a question delivered by my inquisitive five-year-old, "Mom, is it true?" Rather than believing what she was told rote, she began coming home from school asking if certain things she was being told were true.

No. They're not.

Most of what you believe about yourself and your worldview has been handed to you via generational, social, and cultural messaging. These beliefs are a timeless hum that makes up your person. Here's the catch. They will color the world of your children unless you pull that messaging out of you, hold it in your hands, and begin to differentiate between truth and story. It is hard work. You are excavating the old, tragic experiences, the things that go bump in the night, but in the end, the relief is so great. You are left with conscious, purposeful messaging to build up those you love. You are taking off the shine and baring your soul to create healthier paradigms for yourself and your children.

This book pokes at stories, digs holes in belief systems, offers reflection points, and ultimately asks you to love yourself scars and all so you can create a new conversation for yourself and those you influence.

I have spent the last two decades in finance, an unequivocally male-dominated field. As a senior vice president with my firm, an influencer in my community, a philanthropist, and a mom, I have been blessed to meet an army of women who have been on this search with me. We see the gaps in our industries and our cities and look to each other to be voices for those who haven't found theirs. We come together to mentor others, share stories, create dialogue, and most important, build a platform on which women feel comfortable sharing their personal trials and triumphs.

Many of these women have offered their stories and musings and have done the work to show you the way. In these pages, you will find writing and visualization exercises as well as questions to stir up some of the good stuff.

This book has been organized as if you were in a workshop. There are five parts that were informed by an accidental project, Love Letters, that will be referenced many times in this book. Several years ago, I began collecting love letters women wrote to their younger selves and published them on my blog, www.loreandlittlethings.com. I have carefully curated those I think are most salient. The insights were astounding. As I interviewed the writers so I could delve into the stories behind the poetry of their words, themes began to emerge. Those themes are the bones of this book. You will find the exercises build on one another, so have a journal handy.

We begin by unraveling the old; messages from your upbringing and generational and cultural programming in Part I: The Past—Forgive. In Part II: The Present—Choose, we move into the foundation of choice and how your new way forward is based on choosing yourself in all manner of ways and learning to trust yourself. We end our internal work with the future and all that is possible in Part III: The

Future—Manifest. We then move outside ourselves and to the next generation in Part IV: For the Girls. For those who are mothers of boys, I invite you to read through this section as it may provide some insights into ways you can communicate with your sons about the women and girls in their lives. We end with a challenge from the women who wrote letters: my own love letter to my younger self.

Each section has Do the Work Exercises to assist you through free-writing, visualizations, and reflection points. Any time you do deep, internal work, you will need time to process the emotions that bubble to the surface. You may be triggered, you may cry, and you may find yourself stuck on one specific memory or event. Allow for that. Give yourself the time and space to feel through it. Write through it. Do not be afraid of it. You find the truth of self in the excavation of self.

My greatest hope is that every woman who reads this book will find something meant to be whether a quote, a blessing, or a story and will pass it on to the next generation. We are creating our children's lore every day. Our daughters, unfortunately, are suffering from a confidence deficit that keeps them from believing they deserve to be elevated to certain spaces. It comes by way of advertisements, social influence, and generational and cultural messaging.

*The beauty of youth is that they've yet*
*to carry our baggage.*

*—Galit Breen*

How much more powerful could we be if we harnessed our past to reframe our messaging and allow the most harmful messages to die with our generation?

Cycles end every day.

Let's get to work.

The Past // FORGIVE

*We are the stories we tell ourselves.*
—*Joan Didion*

## CHAPTER 1

Uncover YOUR Messaging

T he circumstances of our upbringing and others' comments send us messages that get buried deep in our subconscious and affect everything we do. Every woman who has written a love letter to her younger self knows something intrinsic about herself. When I pointedly ask, "What is one thing you've always known about yourself?" there's barely a pause before adjectives fit for warriors and priestesses are issued with a "Dare you to say I'm not" kind of bravado. These women are determined fighters; they know they have a fire within that cannot be extinguished.

One explained that since the age of five, her father had told her that she had great instincts. She learned how to sharpen the tool she was given, and it created a lifelong relationship with her trust of self. Such a powerful message to grow into knowing deeply that your knowingness would lead you.

When I was a little girl, I knew I was smart. I knew I could get through anything life chucked my way simply because I could brainpower my way through it. I didn't grow up with an innate knowledge that I was intelligent; the messages I received from family members and friends taught me that. They called me the "smart" one. Through conversation and their interest in my little mind, they made it clear I had something going on between my ears. Granted, they referred to my sister as the "cute" one, which created a whole host of self-esteem issues for me, but the point was that this was one of my first messages as a child.

There were other messages though.

"You will spend most of your life believing you are unlovable."

That's the opening line to my love letter to my younger self. When I wrote it, I sucked in my breath and lifted my fingers away from the keys. This hurts, I thought. It hung like a moody cloud over my memories. It wasn't as if anyone had said, "Jeanette, you're clearly unlovable." No. Our negative messaging and conditioning are far more insidious. It became baked into my cells as if in a slow roaster, and I didn't notice until it was too late. Had someone plainly told me I was unlovable, it may have been a blessing. I could have decided right then that I didn't believe that and set up boundaries. Instead, as with most messages we receive, a series of events and unfortunately crafted words created an impression or belief that became as much a thread of the fabric of who I am as is my DNA.

Such messages are far harder to combat and many times much more difficult to decipher as we make our way through life. Even when we uncover them and logically realize they are untrue, they don't just go away; they show up in tragedies, conversations, and life events and are recognized and unwound over and over.

The first step forward is to find them.

I wasn't consciously aware of my struggle with these feelings; this unlovableness, this undeserving nature, until I began digging into my own love letter. The exercise of visualizing your life story requires you to mentally scan the big and sometimes seemingly small (but exponentially powerful) events of your life. It's as if story lines rise to the top and a theme begins to emerge.

First come the big moments, the events that sit within you—a death, a marriage, a divorce, an accident, a birth, the day your heart was broken, or even an event that occurred in a locker room in high school that you can't seem to shake. These visuals and flashes of memory are brighter in color and punch. They get you in the heart and in the gut, but as these colors weave together, you realize they have a similar story line. As you continue, you begin to recall some of the more faded memories—those that are a little gray around the edges or that you've shoved down deep. Over time and after reflection, most have agreed that these colors be they bright and loud or gray, or demonic, slowly become distilled to words as opposed to moments. Words like unlovable, unwanted, forgotten.

When I realized I had not been chosen as a child or shown the love I so deserved and thus had not chosen to love myself, I started sifting through the beginnings. What were the threads that wove this tale of rejection of self? I thought of a time when I was a girl and my mother put all photos of me in our tiny house in a stack in my bedroom. A few days later, I quietly placed my school photo in the living room. I thought Mom might have been over whatever I'd done to make her so angry. I reasoned that maybe one photo wouldn't be so offensive. But that evening, I found the photo back in my room. I couldn't understand why other mothers coveted the jackets full of photos from picture day, but my mother seemed almost repulsed by them.

On another occasion, we were singing in church, and my fingers carefully found my way into my mother's hand. She pushed my hand away and gave me a dirty look. Whenever I reached out to her for affection, she shook me off and snarled, "Get off me!" many times through clenched teeth. The only times my mother's hands were ever on me were to hurt me, rarely out of love.

Later, I dated questionable boys simply because they asked. I didn't think I deserved better. Those small moments as a child continued to show up in my adult relationships. I continued to believe I could get only what was meted out, so I would accept the scraps that were offered. Those scraps eventually turned into abusive relationships and a lot of heartache.

One writer shared that as she scanned all the moments in her life, one continually popped up and finally jarred her. Stephanie's father had attempted suicide many times. After the third failed attempt, she locked herself in the car in the parking lot of the hospital for hours and refused to acknowledge her family's pleadings to unlock the door. Throughout the rest of her life, she had been told that she had nerves of steel and was cool under pressure. The shadow side of that, however, was that she shut herself off from emotion and locked love and relationships out of her life.

Her first line in her letter was, "It's okay to come out of the car." She wrote about the emotional purpose and side effects of those locked doors. "Inside the car, you're safe. No one can hurt you. No one can disappoint you. No one can terrify you, like when those ambulances come in the night and paramedics rush up the steps to take your lifeless-looking dad out on a stretcher."

She explained that locking others out emotionally throughout her life caused devastating trauma to her relationships. She learned to say the words "I love you," but she wouldn't allow herself to actually feel them. The locks that kept out fear also kept out love. She recognizes that the realizations in her letter are part of the key to finally allowing herself to feel these emotions and accepting the inherent risks.

Other women struggled with subconscious messaging; in interviews, they felt uncomfortable talking about specifics. They worried that their mothers or grandmothers would feel as if the resulting body dysmorphia or poor self-esteem was their fault. The matriarchs never expected their judgments of others, their standards of beauty, or their cultural obsessions with food would create decades-long struggles with self-worth and image.

As I surveyed women about body image, I discovered a direct correlation between mothers' feelings toward their bodies and their daughters' struggles with the same. One woman remembered her father warning her to "be careful" so she didn't get big hips and thighs like her mother.

These stories rise to the surface as women work through the Love Letters exercise. When the big tragedies are boiled down, we see that the messages we received as children have created our reactions and self-talk. The seemingly small emotional jabs create stories in us that are untrue. Those jagged scars stitch their way into thick scar tissue, and eventually, we realize that many of the battles we have faced were colored by our impressions of ourselves at the hands and hearts (or lack thereof) of others. Many times, our stories were set in motion much earlier than we thought.

Taking your stories back and unwinding yourself from them offers you the opportunity to change the trajectory of your story line. You get to be creator as opposed to creation, conductor as opposed to note.

You get to step into your power.

**Do the Work**
**Reflection Point**

What events stand out in your mind as you think back to the messaging you received or what you believe about yourself? There are likely more than one. Take this time to write in your journal as they come to mind.

## CHAPTER 2

Finding TRUTH: Belief Systems

The messaging we internalize creates our belief systems. It forms our faith, our impression of gender roles at home and at work, our stance on sexual orientation, and race. They remain in us as baked-in answers and are unwittingly passed along to our children. I didn't realize how lazy I'd become in my own messaging. Enter Olivia.

My daughter, my teacher, has been gifted with a questioning mind, the same one that got me in a ton of trouble as a child. I was considered "willful," but I was never happy with the answers I received. While raised on God and dysfunction by family members who were equal parts godly and alcoholic, I learned to keep myself in check (much more on this in the last chapter, when I share my love letter to my younger self). Because of this, I celebrate my daughter's need to poke holes and her trademark question, "Is that true?"

Olivia recently came home from school to ask if it was true that boys hit you when they liked you. I thought of all the times I'd been told the same and how we needed to do a better job giving boys words because while it may be true in the physical sense, we are also teaching our daughters that being mistreated is a sign of love.

A few days later, she came home and said, "I don't understand this whole 'sticks and stones may break my bones but words will never hurt me' thing. Is that even true?" I had to smile at her sass and explain that no, words can many times hurt you. I thought of all the things we say in a limerick and rhyming fashion and assign clichés and intonations to our conversations hoping they go away without pondering the messaging we are passing down to our children.

So I stole her question and now ask myself often, Is it true? This simple question is a powerful exercise in my workshops; it begins to destabilize negative beliefs. *Thanks, Liv. Mom owes you.*

Is it true that no one will squeeze your hand back with love? Is it true that unlocking the door only lets in chaos? Is it true that if you have broad hips, you're unworthy?

First, we must mine the messaging by pulling it from our subconscious, holding it, and rolling it around in our fingers from a detached position. We have to know what we're dealing with before we can release, change the story line, reprogram ourselves, and mindfully create a new way forward.

After my daughter made me take note of how quickly I was spewing answers in her direction, I started to pause every time she asked me something that might inform her belief system. Then I started taking the same pause in my adult conversations. It made me realize how many of our interactions are riddled with clichés and easy sentences to keep from truly connecting or uncovering our programming.

I finally dug deeply into the things I believed from the time I was a child or struggled with as an adolescent and young adult. I recalled a Bible study when I was maybe twenty. An elder from my congregation quizzically stopped in the middle of the hour-long session, closed his book, and looked at me pointedly and with great concern. "Jeanette, what do you believe?" I didn't realize that as I answered his questions, I started each sentence with, "I was taught to believe …" For the first time, I realized I had no idea what I myself thought. I had been told what to believe my whole life. I didn't know the difference between my parents' thoughts and mine. So began a decades-long search to figure out the difference between faith and fable. I found my way to my free-writing practice to uncover the messages that my conscious mind couldn't see.

My writing practice has become an invaluable part of my life. The best gift I was ever given was a copy of The Artist's Way by Julia Cameron. Ms. Cameron is an expert in what she refers to as creative unblocking. Her works have changed my life. She recommends her morning pages exercise in which you write three pages free-form every morning. It helps unlock the mysteries within. As she says in The Artist's Way workbook, "Morning pages make us known to ourselves." Free-writing is an excellent way to unlock the curiosity that is you. As we work through exercises, please take Ms. Cameron's advice and allow the words to flow unedited. There's magic in the practice.

I personally began to free-write the answers to the question "Is it true?" as I thought through all the messages of my youth. I wanted to dig through my basic belief system, the one that was woven into the fabric of my person before I could raise my hand and have a say in the matter.

Is it true that God is a jealous God? Does He demand retribution for our sins?

Is it true that a woman is to be submissive to a man?

Is it true that sex outside marriage is a sin?

Is it true that homosexuality is a sin?

Is it true that wealth and success are hallmarks of materialism and ego?

Is it true that I have to be small for God to love me?

Your questions may not look exactly like mine; I challenge you to select the beliefs of your upbringing and lay them out. Ask yourself, "Is it true?" and follow it up with, "Do I believe it?"

It was a big no for me on all the above. After many years of searching, I finally found my faith again, but my God, the God I believe in, is not the God of my childhood. He doesn't allow hate in His name. He loves me as I am. I had to dig through the base beliefs I was raised on before I could get to those that were more subtle and present day.

**Do the Work**
**Belief Systems**

Ruminate on your beliefs as a child. Start a sentence with "I believe ..." and let the pen take you where it may. You can use the starter sentences below, one or all, and just write. Write a paragraph. Write until you're done writing. Until the words don't come anymore. Don't edit yourself. The point of free-writing is to engage in a stream of consciousness. Whatever hits the page is what is in your subconscious. That's where the gold is hidden.

- I believe a man's role in the home is to ...

- I believe a woman's role in the home is to ...

- I believe children ...

- I believe in God/divinity/something bigger ...

- I believe in ...

- I believe a woman should look ...

- I believe it's a woman's job to ...

- I believe it's a man's job to ...

- I believe that race is …

- I believe that sexuality is …

After you empty your words onto the page, step back, take a few deep breaths, look over the questions and your responses, and ask yourself, *Is this true? Is this what I believe today?* And if you believe it, ask yourself, *Does it make me feel good?*

## — CHAPTER 3 —

You got it FROM YOUR Mama

Our self-talk is built by a myriad of factors. Some has to do with our mothers' self-talk and how they viewed themselves and their bodies and how they showed up in the world. We received messages from them or our other caregivers very early on in life. They influenced how we see ourselves, take up space, and are viewed by others.

Another factor is how we receive information via advertising, cultural norms, and visual stimulation. A great deal has to do with our self-awareness. Self-talk is the whisper of our otherness. We take it with us wherever we go.

Is yours a friend of foe? I actively try very hard to turn mine into a friend and confront her when she gets all mean-girl on me.

My daughter is usually right under my feet watching my every move. She is often in the bathroom with me when I'm getting ready. One morning as I was putting on my face for the day, she rifled through my makeup drawer and held up my mascara as if it were a treasure. "What is this?" she asked. I caught myself before I said the first thing that came to mind, which was, "It makes Mommy's eyes look pretty. I can't go out in public without it because Mom has no pigment in her face."

Umm, no. Time out, Mom.

There was absolutely no self-love or worthiness coming out of the drawer that holds the paints I hide my face behind each day in the hopes of oddly enough being seen. I wondered if the messages I received about the way I painstakingly prepared for the day were true and how I had gotten to the place where all my pretty is in a drawer. Does my worth lie at the bottom of a bottle of MAC foundation NWA15 so much so that I am scared to leave home without suffocating my pores in the quest for perfection?

Olivia asked me recently, "Mommy, why do you wear makeup every day?" The first thing that came to mind was, "Mommy wants a boyfriend," but I just laughed to myself and took the pause that has become standard for us when I dig through my messaging before I build hers. "Makeup helps make our features stand out a little more. I like to wear mascara because it makes my eyes look even brighter than they are."

The messaging of my youth about body and self has been hard to shake. I was told that if I hugged a man, he would think I wanted to have sex. If my dress was too revealing, I was telling him I was open to sex. If I wore too much makeup, I was letting him know I was a Jezebel and would likely have sex. Anything and everything I did could make a man want to have sex with me, which would pretty much be my fault, so *Hide yourself, girl. Don't you know what you do to them?* I started wearing yoga pants outside my house (and a yoga class) only this year, and it was on a dare and simply because I had a four-hour flight. *Oh my God, they're so comfortable!*

We have to learn to monitor our thoughts, understand where they came and come from, and how to make friends with them. It takes time to unravel what has become a hum in our veins, but self-observation is a mighty tool in recreating our inner self-talk. We do it for our own self-worth and that of the next generation we are influencing.

**Do the Work**
**Self-Talk**

Many women I've interviewed have shared that their mothers' self-talk about their bodies became their self-talk. A parent's refusal to discuss sex or puberty became shame, and it gave the impression that women were for the pleasure of men. I'm the first person to admit I struggle in this area. I would love to say that I am enlightened and don't need makeup or heels, that I'm free, but that would be untrue. I consciously know that my worth is not in my body, but subconsciously, I struggle with self-esteem. Show me a woman who doesn't and I'll show you a corpse.

I have found that I no longer consciously feel shame about my curves or lend credence to the prevalent rape-culture mentality that said women were to blame for men's bad behavior. But that was only because I had overhauled my own messaging.

- How has your early messaging shaped your beliefs and self-talk?

- What do you tell yourself when no one else is listening? Is it true?

- What do you tell yourself when you look in the mirror? Is it true?

- How do images of women in ads, movies, and social media affect your self-talk?

- Is it true that a woman's worth is her body?

- Is it true that women are for the pleasure of men?

- Is it true that a woman should be a certain size or stature to be considered beautiful?

- Is it true that a woman has to strive for physical perfection to "get and keep her man?"

— CHAPTER 4 —

# Tragic LIFE Events

*Sometimes in tragedy we find our life's purpose.*
*The eye sheds a tear to find its focus.*
—*Robert Brault*

T ragedy strikes us all in a variety of ways. It could be the death of a loved one, an accident, an illness, or violence. Many speak of the anger they feel. Some leave their faith, and others find it again. Most speak of there being a before and an after when referring to the event and how it has influenced their lives.

I have experienced a variety of trauma in my life that has shaped my outcome. In their moments, they were very hard in their own way. I couldn't breathe. I couldn't sleep. I had aching feelings in my chest, insomnia, tremors. After one traumatic event, I lay on my bedroom floor sobbing. I couldn't get out of my pain. It consumed me as if it had no end. I couldn't imagine a life off that floor while I was in the thickness of my hurt.

Eventually, I found my footing again and vowed to use my pain as opposed to becoming it.

One of the breathtaking things about speaking to women who have experienced trauma and used it to serve them, as opposed to letting it break them, is their tireless advocacy for self and their ironclad boundaries. They have come out of fire and have been forged with iron breastplates and superhuman BS detection systems. They know themselves inside and out. They know their triggers. They know what they will stand for and what they will not. They become voices for those who have experienced the same pain, and they turn their stories into lessons. In as much as they heal others, they heal themselves.

Once while I was hosting a workshop, I was asked what the most profound message I had received from the writers was. I broke out in goose bumps. I channeled the image of Chelli Wolford, an entrepreneur and sister to recording artist Pitbull at age forty speaking to her four-year-old self, the age she was when her uncle began molesting her. Her message? "It's not your fault."

It took Chelli three decades to release the blame she felt for the trajectory of her life. She finally realized that we don't control others' bad behavior and that a four-year-old girl should never carry such burdens. I felt the energy in the room shift as I shared her story. Several women cried. Afterward, a handful of women thanked me for sharing her words. They were the same words they were struggling with at that time.

Chelli was gang-raped her freshman year at the Naval Academy by four or five men; she's never been sure of the number. In her interview, she shared that the act was a blur, but she vividly remembers sitting on the floor of her closet after the attack with an X-Acto knife to her wrist and thinking, *This happened to you because you can handle it.* She never reported the rape. She spent two weeks at the naval hospital in Bethesda for what was believed to have been an attempted suicide. The resulting pregnancy and abortion were also handled alone. She went back to school the next day.

For Chelli, a child who had been abandoned by her mother when she was just eighteen months old, the Naval Academy was her way out of a traumatic childhood. She couldn't imagine going back to her life in an Ohio junkyard. She graduated, but the attack and its repercussions lived on in her.

She later realized that it affected the relationships she entered and her self-esteem. When she decided that sitting in the darkness and continuing a pattern of abusive relationships was not the way she wanted to continue, the real work began. She had to feel the pain and work through the trauma. She has become a beautiful voice in self-empowerment, women's rights, and advocacy for foster children and victims of domestic violence. I encourage you to watch her interview. It's stunning. You'll find her letter to her younger self in these pages.

On the same day I interviewed Chelli, I interviewed Adrianne Haslet, ballroom dancer, activist, and survivor of the Boston Marathon bombing. Adrianne wrote a love letter to her younger self prior to losing her leg, but she has struggled to complete the love letter she is working on after the events of April, 2013. She believes passionately in emotional honesty, and she graciously explained that she challenged herself to show up without the letter and talk about why it was hard for her to write.

While most women picture themselves at a specific age and speak to that girl, Adrianne can't resolve the fact that in her new body, she feels five years old. That was a profound realization. A senseless act of violence changed her body, nearly ruined her professional career as a dancer, and affected this incredibly strong woman's emotional outlook. She speaks openly about post-traumatic stress and the ways we misunderstand it: "You think it's supposed to get better the further out you are from it, but it doesn't."

Adrianne is aware of her triggers. She avoids fireworks, stressful situations, and overly packed schedules. She practices self-care, establishes very important boundaries—for others and herself—and is an active participant in her healing. She speaks all over the world about her experiences of overcoming challenges and advocating for amputees' rights. She recently opened and closed Vancouver Fashion Week for up-and-coming designer Lesley Hampton, who is building her career celebrating women's bodies in all their iterations.

Perhaps most impressive is that Adrianne has danced again, something she decided in the moments following the attack. She has also taken up running and recently completed the Boston Marathon on a carbon-fiber blade.

These women would tell you to feel your pain and be one with it but in a way that moves you through it and gets you to the other side. Your pain must not become your identity. You are so much bigger than that, and you have many more lives to touch and experiences to create. Become your own best advocate whether that means working with a therapist or a healer. Free-write until your hands cramp and your heart is bleeding onto the page. Join a support group. Join a nunnery. Learn tapping. Only you can chart the course of your healing, so be open to whatever form that takes. Hold your trauma in your hands, and know that one day you will realize it did something for you.

**Do the Work**
**Self-Care**

If you have experienced tragedy, find yourself triggered, or need a moment, please take this time to turn to your self-care. Be gentle. Tread lightly. Love yourself. Consider what you can do to become a better caregiver to yourself.

## CHAPTER 5

*Forgiveness is the final form of love.*
*—Reinhold Niebuhr*

*"Come now, let us settle the matters" says the LORD. "Though*
*your sins are like scarlet, they shall be white as snow; though*
*they are red as crimson, they shall be like wool."*
*—Isaiah 1:18*

*Someone must risk returning injury with kindness,*
*or hostility will never turn to goodwill.*
*—Tao Te Ching verse 79*

F orgiveness is simple in theory, but it is a concept covered by every walk of life, culture, and religion because it is difficult in practice. It is offered to us in the Bible as a blessing from God, but in our own lives, it's almost as impossible as the pursuit of balance is. We carry people and events with us as if they've taken up space in our bodies and minds, and they taint our actions. We allow them to frame our worldview, and we shake our head at their actions, yet they've gone on to live their lives. The only person still affected is the one who has yet to forgive.

I've studied a number of forgiveness rituals; the Navajo and Hawaiian rituals stand out because of their compassion and simplicity. They show how lightly we can approach forgiveness. If you want to burn photos or write angry letters, which we'll get to, do so. Sometimes, we have to punch things to get someone out of us, but the beauty and wisdom of those who came before us is something to acknowledge. In the end, forgiveness is grace.

The Navajo forgiveness ritual allows for the hearing of a grievance by tribal elders. The wounded party sits with the members of his or her tribe. The tribe holds space while the story is told a total of three times. The one with a grievance is offered hearing ears and compassion. However, if the grievance is shared a fourth time, the tribal members turn their backs on the one seeking an ear as if to say, "Enough. Let it go. It is you who is now carrying this with you."

The Hawaiian forgiveness ritual of Ho'oponopono is a beautiful practice of compassion. It is built on the premise that we are all connected and that anything to be forgiven in you must also have root in me. There are four simple sentences you repeat as a mantra while holding the event or individual in mind: I'm sorry. Please forgive me. I love you. Thank you.

Synonyms for forgiveness include mercy, compassion, and clemency, but when you delve into the practice of radical forgiveness, author Colin Tipping in a book by the same name, suggests that there was never a grievance to begin with. This theory allows you to remove yourself from the place of victimhood. He argues that the offender has contracted with you on a soul level to act as a guide and the source of the lesson. While many who have experienced crushing and tragic events have a particularly hard time imagining they would ever contract violence or loss, he asks the reader to be open to the concept as they read and not necessarily adopt it but allow for it to be a possibility.

No matter your view of forgiveness on the spiritual or practical spectrum, if you choose to stop being wounded, if you stop allowing the stories and sins of others to mark your life, you take center stage and once again are the creator of your path. You came into this life alone and will leave alone, so why carry the burden of another throughout the span of that time line?

By forgiving, we choose not to waste any more energy identifying with and becoming consumed by the happenings of the past. That allows us to choose what we give our attention to as opposed to falling into unconscious patterns and ways of relating. But it isn't easy. It requires intention and action, and many times, it's a slow process.

Whenever I think of forgiveness, I have a vision of Iyanla VanZant on stage in San Jose a few years ago. She was giving a talk on forgiveness. If there were a mythological Greek name for her, it would translate Goddess of Forgiveness. I sat transfixed as she talked about forgiving her ex-husband and his new partner, her former best friend. She had every reason to be angry, to feel betrayed, but instead, she actively practiced forgiveness. She forgave him each day rather than sitting in anger and bitterness. Even on the days she hated him, she would repeat her mantra, "I forgive you," until it was true. Forgiveness wasn't for him. It was for her.

Forgiveness is for you. People don't often do things because they don't like you or because you're bad. They do things because of what they have experienced before you. A way to promote compassion and move toward forgiveness is to imagine the people you are at odds with having thought clouds behind their heads. In those clouds are all the stories, interactions, and tragedies they have encountered. All those swirling, bubbling memories influence their output.

A very simple example of this was a recent encounter I had with an executive at my firm. I asked her to meet a client, and she booked a flight from New York to Las Vegas. Pre-planning was done and confirmations made, but while she was on the plane, the client canceled for reasons that no one expected and were out of our control. I quickly arranged another meeting for her so her trip wouldn't be useless. While I felt bad that she had made such a long trip, I also knew it wasn't my fault and wanted to make her visit as comfortable as possible.

When she came into the office the next day, I saw fury on her face. It was unnatural anger, and as she blamed me and made it clear she found the situation to be annoying and infuriating, I was confident that I could not have possibly caused that much anger. I imagined the thought cloud behind her head and knew it included a fear of flying and two children at home. In that moment, I felt compassion for her and realized she wasn't aware of how unnatural her venom toward me was. She may never. I realized that pointing it out would not work to my advantage in that heated moment, so I smiled, neutralized the situation, and excused myself.

Allowing ourselves to imagine the thought cloud each of us walks into every situation with can offer us perspective. We have the opportunity to gain footing as we internally refocus our energy from a place of defense to a place of observation and respect for self and others.

Compassion for another does not mean allowing yourself to be walked on, or reentering a toxic relationship because you understand someone better, or relinquishing boundaries because they are flawed or troubled. No. Compassion and forgiveness frees you, not the other.

They are simply to help you regain perspective and allow you to heal and rewrite your story without the smudged memories of the other.

This practice is not a one-and-done type of thing. Expressing compassion or practicing forgiveness in the moment is helpful, but that doesn't always stick as we find that our storied lives and triggers come in layers. There may be some relationships that require active forgiveness, as Iyanla demonstrated, until the burden is lighter, the soul feels freer, and you have cut the cord. Set the intention of forgiveness each day, and send that intention on its way with blessings and forgiveness in prayer or meditation. Do that until you forget to do it one day. Do it until it's no longer on your mind or heart.

Forgiveness is like grief. You go through it in stages and experience it in layers. Each person is different in how they experience it and how they heal. Some hurt is easily released. You may wince a little in the remembering, but no active emotion is attached. There will be other times when you feel you've healed completely but are suddenly triggered. Lighting sage, saying a prayer, or creating intentions doesn't always cut it. Sometimes, you have to physically release it.

I have done exhaustive work to actively forgive my ex-husband, his family, and the details of our divorce. We spend holidays together, and we have a wonderful coparenting relationship. He is a present parent, a good father, and I adore his girlfriend. I was so proud of how far I'd come and what an emotionally resilient mother I could be. *Yay me!*

Then one day, his father was visiting for our daughter's birthday and an old pattern arose. It was something I'd not experienced for several years. He asked our daughter if she'd rather stay with me or "come with your family," emphasis on the word family. Olivia's cousin had obviously heard that before, and she asked my daughter with a hint of disdain, "Do you even like being with your mom?" It knocked me back to the days we were ending our marriage. His family quickly closed ranks, and I truly understood the expression that blood is thicker than water.

The interaction triggered me. It brought out an unnatural response. Anyone looking in from the outside might have rolled his or her eyes at the behavior—Yeah, it's annoying, but just ignore it—or told me to stand up for myself, but the anger I felt didn't match the situation. It was an unhealthy, deep-seated anger that needed to be uprooted. Had I reacted in the moment, you would have seen a mushroom cloud over a suburban home in Las Vegas.

I had to get away from it and breathe through it, but it didn't leave me. I found myself mentioning it to friends, and I was suddenly edgier even in my interactions at work. I'd allowed the anger to spread, and I knew enough about myself to realize I hadn't fully forgiven my ex's family. The interaction was simply opening a much deeper wound. So I called my friend Gaylynn, a personal trainer with a professional boxing lineage, and told her I needed to beat some anger out; I asked if she would help me. She designed a series of workouts that were aggressive in nature and allowed me to punch, throw, kick, and strike. I threw balls to the ground with controlled fury. No one else in the gym knew what we were up to, but there I was taped up, visualizing the things that were on my mind, and beating the ever-living hell out of whatever she put in front of me.

Various interactions with family members throughout the course of my divorce began to surface as I pounded my anger out. Gaylynn offered instructions, but when the look was intense and the jabs powerful, she stayed present while I worked it out. She'd stop counting me down, a silent understanding between us. Inevitably, I would suddenly tire and bend from the waist to catch my breath or find myself walking off the exhaustion. I had the energy to expend my pure rage. When I'd forgiven that moment or that person, I didn't have it in me anymore.

Gaylynn, a God-fearing woman, always said a sweet prayer for me as she stretched me out at the end of our sessions. I left feeling lighter, freer, and more in control of the me I had been missing while I had walked around with my misplaced anger. I pushed that story out of me one jab and one right hook at a time.

One woman shared that for her to forgive, she has to beat a pillow to remove the event from the memory bank of her body. Another puts Brene Brown on Audible and imagines the hurt child in the other. Another shared that she uses meditation to retrace the event and understand where she stepped out of integrity and behaved in ways that she knew weren't up to her standards. She is then able to realize the lesson, the radical forgiveness required.

I ask a brief grouping of questions in every workshop I facilitate. One is, "Whom do you need to forgive?" Several people wipe tears away, look down, and will themselves strong. I almost always feel a change in the energy in the room. After giving a few moments of reflection, I follow it up with "Is that person you?" The soft sobs become audible, which makes me wonder if forgiveness isn't a key. Could it possibly unlock us, unchain us from our past? Could we create an active forgiveness practice that truly exorcises the demons that haunt us? Those we choose to avoid or still allow to walk with us?

We wrap our lives around the sins of others, and they in turn affect us on a go-forward basis. They never truly lose their influence over us if we don't actively make the decision to forgive them. Before we can forgive, we have to acknowledge our part many times. With the exception of violent acts and criminal behavior, we are not victims or martyrs. Those are unbecoming traits that keep us locked in the power of the offender. To fully forgive self and others, we must first take responsibility for our part in the pain. It is a toxic thing to throw all the blame and bitterness on another. Move further away from it and look at it from a broader perspective. Could we have behaved differently? Where did we fall short? Did we fall out of integrity and perhaps allow behavior because of our issues with self-esteem and inappropriate boundaries? Could compassion be utilized in our forgiveness exercise? Could we, as author Shaka Senghor teaches, see the injured child in another?

If the person to be forgiven is you, I offer that self-love is your friend. Be gentle with yourself. Offer yourself the same compassion, and recognize that you also have been programmed. The first step forward in your new life involves excavating and forgiving. The exercises in this book will allow you to hold yourself in a space of gratitude and acceptance. They may help you reframe certain actions and belief systems so you can see yourself through a wiser, more exacting lens. Be excited about the opportunity to move to the creative and purposeful stage of your life, and thank your younger self for the life lessons. She has served you well; she has gotten you to this place of self-awareness and actualization. She can't be all bad.

## Do the Work
### The Intention of Forgiveness

It would be disingenuous to suggest that you can simply say, "All is forgiven," with a wave of the hand in the throes of pain. Forgiveness is a practice, not a quick and final action. You can start on the path to forgiveness, however, by setting the intention to forgive. Create a forgiveness mantra, something you can defer to or even meditate on as you practice active forgiveness.

I was once very hurt by a man I loved. It took me two years to think of him without becoming irritated or angry. In that resentment, I knew I had to find my way to forgiveness. I tucked a mantra in the notes function of my phone so I could refer to it as I tried to finally let his power over me go: "I am willing to look at you with compassion and forgiveness."

Here's a more powerful verse to try: "I intend to forgive this experience and all involved."

Write a forgiveness mantra that feels appropriate to you and your situation.

- I intend …

- It is my intention to …

**Do the Work**
**Hot Letters**

There is brilliance in the art of the unsent angry letter. Abraham Lincoln called them hot letters. I've had the honor of hearing historian Doris Kearns Goodwin several times as she shared stories of the letters Lincoln would write to his commanders, most interestingly one to General George G. Meade in which he blamed him for Robert E. Lee's escape after Gettysburg. Lincoln would unleash all his emotions into the letter, set it aside until his emotions cooled down, and then later write on it, "Never sent. Never signed."

I believe this is a wonderful opportunity to use the gut-check method I swear I'm going to have trademarked. It gives you permission to simply listen to your body. As you think of an individual or begin to write to that person, does your pulse race? Do you become agitated? Do you pace? Do tears form? Do you clench your jaw? These are physical manifestations of unchecked emotions. Believe them. Allow them to be unleashed on the page until the words no longer flow. Then step away from them. Give them time to bleed out of you and onto the paper.

# Part I Key Takeaways

- Define your messaging. Make it separate from you while you examine what you have been told versus what you believe to be true.

- Uncover your religious, cultural, and social biases. Dig in and find your truth.

- Excavate the messaging you received as a child about your worth, self-image, and values; examine the way they have set the stage for your relationships with self and others.

- Change the conversation that occurs when you look in the mirror.

- Review the trauma and tragic life events that have shaped your story. Can you find a blessing or a lesson?

- Create your own forgiveness practice. Forgive actively. Purposefully. For you.

— Chapter **6** —

# The Letters:
## FORGIVING
# The Past

**N**o one realized how much work the letters would be when we began. Women raised their hands hoping to inspire others by showing how alike we are, and then at some point, they each said some variation of "Wow, that was really hard" or "That was therapy I wasn't expecting." Everyone referred to it as a powerful practice they would continue.

The first letter I received was from Emmy Award–winning WCBS New York weekend anchor Jessica Moore. At the time, she was the evening anchor for NBC affiliate KTNV in Las Vegas. We'd met three years earlier through our mutual friend, Fox Sports reporter Jamie Little. Jessica and I became fast friends who bonded over failed relationships. We joked that Jamie was running an unofficial halfway house for the heartbroken, both of us having stayed in her guest house while we each moved from partnered to party of one.

Roughly a year after we met and when we were both further away from heartbreak and sipping drinks on one of our many weekend retreats, I found myself saying aloud, "I want to write love letters to women and girls." But I had no idea what that meant or where it would lead. I simply felt so much wisdom could be shared, and I wanted to create space for women to help one another.

I'd recently become involved in the Gender Lens movement, and my brain was rife with some mind-boggling stats. I ate up data for days from the Kennedy School's Social Innovation and Change Initiative at Harvard, and I followed the very thoughtful activism of Pax Ellevate, a fund company that votes their proxies against any company that has fewer than two women on its board.

With women making up only 4 percent of the C suite, being 33 percent of senior leadership roles, earning 20 percent less for the same work, and still outperforming their peers in each industry, it's clear there's something preventing the ascension of women into leadership roles, and I was ready to root out the reasons. We are a better economy and society for it, and we finally have data to prove it. Are men keeping women from equality at the highest levels? This is highly plausible depending on the industry. Are women of their own volition holding themselves back? Sadly, the answer is a big, loud, dirty yes.

Something appears to happen to girls at a young age that makes them believe at their core that they don't belong or don't deserve to be in certain elevated spaces. As daughter grows into potential decision maker, a confidence deficit suffocates her possibilities and potential. You don't have to look far to find studies on adolescent and teenage girls confirming that the most glaring issues are those of self-esteem, social influence, messaging, and mentorship.

As a writer, my first inclination was to pen more articles, but the last thing the world needs is more articles about how we're failing our gender. I wanted to find an attractive way to present viral mentorship, and as always, the answers lie in ourselves. I just needed a lot of selves to be willing to share their learnings, fears, and failures and commit them to paper. I wanted moms and daughters to read these words together. I also knew based on Jessica's letter and because of many years of writing, that women could frame letters to their younger selves to help identify issues in their pasts that may have dampened their self-esteem and confidence and inhibited them from achieving their true aspirations.

Like many women before me, I faced issues of worth as I built out the project. Who am I to write a letter? I'm a nobody. This thought would continue to show up in conversations in which very wise women would call me out and brazenly force an intervention or three when we discussed my issues with self-esteem and childhood messaging. I didn't know I would meet these damn feelings head-on when I started this adventure. *This is for the girls. Why are we talking about me?* Yet I'm dredging them up and tucking them into the notes function of my phone, so I can ruminate on them prior to weaving them into the structured sentences of my letter.

When Jessica's letter appeared in my inbox, tears snaked their way down my cheeks. The words had been thoroughly thought through with care and rendered in a tender tone. I expected solutions, bullet points, and "You got this, girl," not fully understanding the emotional appeal of these letters. To her credit, Jessica showed me her heart, and I knew I was onto something big. I decided to roll the dice. With no other love letters in hand, I published it on my blog the following week with a dare to the universe—If I publish it, they will come.

The universe did not disappoint. Shortly after that, I was overwhelmed by letters and emails from readers. Jessica, Jamie, and I met for drinks one night. As Jess sat, her face solemn, I could tell she had been touched by the outpouring of private messages and soulful conversations she hadn't expected. "This was needed. Women need this honesty from each other," she said. Her lack of another clarifying sentence was perfect. She was stunned, and I knew this project was going to be bigger and more beautiful than I had imagined.

Jessica's letter started a small movement. The weekend after it was published, she emceed a charity event in Las Vegas. Women came up to both of us to share some of their own misgivings and wonder aloud, "Why don't we talk about these things more? Why are we so hard on each other and ourselves?"

More letters rolled in, and they were published and read by curious and hopeful eyes. But as they arrived touting different stories and voices, deeper conversations followed about the process and what it accomplished for the writers themselves. I began interviewing the writers on camera for a webisode series; I dug into the stories behind the beautiful words. At times, they would suddenly tear up or become reflective. At times, I could tell that something big had occurred while the cameras were rolling, but it typically wasn't until we'd have dinner afterward that writers would explain what I felt so intuitively. More often than not, they would share that there was something they were healing from that moment or had realized they needed to look deeper into the triggers.

Each meal after an on-camera interview looks the same. We're grateful but very tired. The writers have willfully dug into their pasts originally to help others and suddenly realize how much they are helping themselves. They feel raw but happy, and I see the marks of relief on their cheeks. I am typically almost facedown in whatever I'm eating or toasting. The focus required to give women the platform and respect they need to share these truths is steely, measured, and exhausting. I am protective of them as we film the interviews and even prior to their letters being published. I ask them over and over if there are any no-fly zones—areas they're not ready to share.

My exhaustion and celebration after interviews proves to me that the words have been blessed with genuine care and concern. They are not flung into the wind or leveled over by a marketing team. What you see in an interview and on a page is heart, soul, and conviction—theirs, mine, and eventually those of the women reading them as they soak in the messages meant for them.

These letters follow. I hope they touch and inspire you as they have me and so many others. They may begin to frame your thoughts, memories, and words as you construct the foundation of your letter. After all, after bearing witness to the mining of so much personal truth, I'm finally ready to write my letter.

Are you ready to write yours?

Let's do this, ladies. Together. Let's learn from our sisters, our mothers, and more important, ourselves. That's where the answers are. You just have to tap into your inner voice, your subconscious, and I'll help you do that in our time together. I hope that when you're done inking your story, you recognize the beauty within that you may have forgotten, the strengths you take for granted, the memories you can release, and the grit that resides in your souls.

I'm in this with you.

I selected this group of letters specifically because each writer reflects on past events and traumas and their healing journeys. What they write is raw—and fair warning—may trigger those who have experienced sexual assault. I thank them from the bottom of my heart for trusting this platform to share their stories.

# Chelli Wolford

Earlier, I introduced you to Chelli Wolford, who survived abandonment and sexual violence to become a heroine among women. This is her powerful later to her younger self, version #27.

My Dearest Chelli-Belly:

(That nickname is going to stick, but you'll eventually find it endearing.)

First, and I need you to really get this like in your cells, know this: It's not your fault. Your mother leaving you when you were just a baby. Being molested when you were a child. Getting gang-raped your first year of college. None of it was your fault. It will be easy for you to blame yourself, to shame and convince yourself that it was somehow your fault, that you were being punished, that, God forbid, you deserved it. Sweetheart, it just wasn't your fault. Stop asking why, and start looking to transform your pain into purpose. This is how you will find peace and become of service to the world.

Learn to forgive as if it were your job. Forgive those who have hurt you, and forgive yourself for those you have hurt. Forgiveness is freedom. Learn to live intentionally and you won't need to ask for forgiveness near as often. Everything will fall into place.

*When people show you who they really are, believe them the first time.*
—*Maya Angelou*

People will give you all the information you need to make decisions about whether you should allow them into your life and heart. Not only will they show you; sometimes, they will also tell you. Don't think you can love them better. You can't. Don't justify bad behavior. When they show you who they really are, believe them.

Marry the kind guy you think is too good for you. That will change the trajectory of your life. Having a supportive partner who will assist in your becoming will be everything.

Some things are never going to make sense, but that's okay. Your mother not choosing you will perplex you most of your life. Instead of asking why, just know that she did the best she could with the tools she had. You will do better because you will know firsthand what it feels like to be left behind. It will take you a little while, but eventually, you will see your curses as blessings. Your worst days will become your best days that will shape you into a wildly compassionate woman.

You don't need to prove yourself to anyone. Full stop.

I'm not going to lie to you—the first several years will be challenging, but my love, it will get so sweet. The darkness will diminish. You will see only the light. Your heart will grow. You will laugh way more than you cry. You will experience things that you cannot imagine right now as you lie in your bed in a junkyard in Ohio dreaming big dreams for yourself. Hold on. You're worth it.

Finally, thank you for being a brave, badass, risk-taking, young girl. You got me here. But now, I got you. I'm holding you tight. You are safe, and you can trust me completely. You can be vulnerable and soft and feminine. I will not judge you. Cry if you need to cry, say your scary things out loud, be your most authentic self. I will be with you every day until we die, and I will forever be your biggest fan. You saved me. And I saved you. It will take you a few years, but you will realize I'm the love of your life.

So much love and light to you,

Chelli

*Chelli Wolford is a strategic business consultant who combines over twenty years of experience in the military, business, and entertainment worlds. She was the youngest and only female retail sales manager for Sprint PCS when she moved to Las Vegas at age twenty-four; she built five retail stores in the Las Vegas market and managed nearly a hundred employees. She quickly advanced; she managed several sales channels in multiple organizations and became known as a fixer—someone who could turn around flailing sales channels through key position hires, team building, and a leading-by-example style of management.*

*After leaving the corporate world, Chelli was chosen by international superstar Pitbull to join his team and help take his organization to the next level. She created processes for vetting business opportunities; she delineated clear roles for team members in the Pitbull organization and worked closely with Pitbull, aka Armando Perez, to ensure that his brand was consistent throughout his social channels and that he had a direct, authentic connection to his fans to ensure channel growth.*

*During this time, Chelli cofounded Acento Digital Media, a company that supported and connected music artists and brands in aligned, mutually beneficial relationships. Acento's revenue grew to half a million in less than four years of business.*

*Chelli recently moved back to Las Vegas after eight years in California and focuses on empowering women entrepreneurs to achieve their goals through her new company, Illuminated Moxie.*

# Caroline Heldman

Caroline Heldman is a force, a whirlwind, and pure soul. She utilizes her platform as a political correspondent, researcher, associate professor, and activist to raise her voice for those who are unable. I was honored that she agreed to include her love letter for this project.

Dear Little Caroline,

I want you to know that violent storms are coming and that no one can save you but yourself.

As a child, you will be beaten, and no one will protect you. It will start so young that you will think it's just the way it is. It will happen more times than you can count, so you will stop counting.

When you are raped the first time, no one will help you and no one will believe you. You will confide in an adult you trust, but she will shame you and tell you it was your fault though you're only four. But you know in your core that it is not your fault, so you learn not to rely on adults to save you.

When you are sixteen, you will run away from home after being strangled by a sibling. A man will come to rescue you, but he will take you to his house and rape you. The next morning, he will serve you scrambled eggs on a black plate and tell you that no one will believe you. He is right. The police tell you it is a he said–she said situation even though he is twenty-eight. This is painful at the time, but it will teach you not to rely on institutions to save you.

This experience will leave you homeless, so you will live in your car while you finish up community college. You'll work hard to be elected student body president so you will have an office to sleep in. You'll wake up early and use the shower in the gym before anyone gets there. You have already learned to go hungry for days on end from a childhood of hunger, so the day-old donuts in the college bakery will become a daily staple.

By the time you're in your late teens, you will have learned to save yourself. You will be able to go days without eating much because you've had to just to survive. You will have spent years in martial arts training your body to deflect and withstand serious violence. Vicious blows no longer scare you. You will have become accustomed to getting only a few hours of sleep a night so you can work full time to put yourself through college. You have taken out tens of thousands of dollars in student loans because you don't believe you will live past thirty. But you will live.

After college, you will hop on your first plane and relocate to Washington, DC, to work for congress with only $124 in your pocket. You fear nothing because you know you can survive just about anything. You will earn a PhD while living below the poverty line because your hunger for insight and independence is so much stronger than your hunger for food.

One day, you will wake up and realize you have a prestigious job, a reliable car, and clothes without rips or stains. You can afford all the food you want because you make more money than you know what to do with. You will always buy your clothes and cars secondhand because money means nothing to you beyond survival.

When you no longer have to fight so hard to survive, you will feel deep pangs of guilt at your comfort. You will turn that guilt into activism. As Alice Walker put it, "Activism is my rent to living on the planet."

You will advocate for girls like you who have been raped, for women who are homeless, for poor people who are dehumanized. You will fight against the people and institutions that betray the vulnerable. You will sacrifice your reputation and your career for causes, and you will do so without fear because this world cannot hurt you more than you have already been hurt.

When you are older, you will look back and grieve the loss of your childhood, your family, and your lack of faith in most humans.

But you will not be a sad person. You will be a grateful warrior who looks for the next meaningful fight. "Fate whispers to the warrior, 'You cannot withstand the storm,' and the warrior whispers back, 'I am the storm.'"

Love,


Caroline


*Dr. Heldman is an associate professor of politics at Occidental College in Los Angeles and the research director for the Geena Davis Institute for Gender in Media. Her research specializes in media, the presidency, and systems of power (race, class, gender). Dr. Heldman coedited Rethinking Madame President: Are We Ready for a Woman in the White House? (Lynne Rienner, 2007) and authored Protest Politics in the Marketplace: Consumer Activism in the Corporate Age (Cornell University Press, 2017), Women, Power, and Politics: The Fight for Gender Equality in the United States (Oxford University Press, 2017), The New Campus Anti-Rape Movement (Lexington, 2018), and Gender and Resistance in the 2016 Presidential Election (Praeger, 2018).*

*Dr. Heldman has been active in real-world politics as a professional pollster, campaign manager, and commentator for CNN, MSNBC, FOX News, and CNBC. She has also been featured in popular documentaries including Missrepresentation, The Mask You Live In, The Hunting Ground, Informant, Equal Means Equal, and Liberated.*

*Dr. Heldman was one of many women who went public with allegations of gender discrimination against Bill O'Reilly that led to his firing from Fox News. She splits her time between Los Angeles and New*

Orleans, where she cofounded the New Orleans Women's Shelter and the Lower Ninth Ward Living Museum. Dr. Heldman also cofounded End Rape on Campus (EROC), Faculty Against Rape (FAR), and End Rape Statute of Limitations (ERSOL).

a

# Camille DiMaio

Author Camille DiMaio is mother to three wonderful young women and one lucky young man. I often find myself turning to Camille's words and conscious approach to life, love, and the English language.

Dear Younger Camille,

It will take you months to write this letter. Not the actual words. You will type those out in minutes. But it will take longer to commit to them, curate them, share them.

Because it's not a simple thing to bleed onto paper.

I will tell you the end first, or at least the end as it sits here at age forty, which once seemed like an unimaginable ancientness to you. The end is good. Very good. And you've found only two gray hairs, so four decades really isn't as decrepit as you think.

But if there are more, you will have earned them.

You won't have a friend until you're fourteen. You will have vampire-like teeth and Coke-bottle glasses and be picked last in gym class. The girls in seventh grade will write a public declaration of dislike. You'll become the reclusive kid who spends all the time in the library. Your friends will all be fictional, and their names will be Nancy

Drew, Anne Shirley, Jane Eyre, and Christine Daae. You will live in their worlds and pore over their words.

You will fall in love with a guy who tells you that he slept with someone behind your back because he couldn't wait for you any longer. You will spend years convinced that you are worth only the sum of your female parts.

You will love the theater, but you will be cast as a chorus girl time after time. You will accept that you are not the one with the most talent, but you will enthusiastically support the show with your bit-part contribution. But one day, you will audition for a lead role and your performance with your partner will be so moving that the other people auditioning will give you both a standing ovation. And yet neither of you will get even a small role in the production because of the director's personal friendship with the eventual leading lady. (Who by the way will grimace when she has to kiss the leading man.)

You will be assaulted by someone you tried to be nice to when no one else was. He will wait until you are alone and will press you against a wall and try to force something on you that you don't want, even rubbing hundreds of dollars in cash against your cheek as an offering. You will get away physically intact but emotionally scarred. You will tell the police, who will say they can't do anything since there is no evidence.

It will be more than a decade before you can hear the words Dominican Republic without shuddering because that's where he was from.

You will move across the country after a devastating period of unemployment. You will be hospitalized with a serious illness during which you will almost lose your unborn baby. You will be threatened by someone who tells you he will kill your children. You will mourn the suicide of someone in your family. You will have a chronic health issue that often makes your days painful.

But you will emerge very strong.

The bullying will teach you to be kind. The cheating will teach you to be loyal. The loss of the lead role will teach you to never give up. The attack will teach you to defend yourself. All of it—every moment that seemed bad at the time—will be a lesson that will build your character, fortitude, and faith.

And there will be good moments. Oh will there ever be! You will ride on a camel in front of a pyramid. You will meet Mother Teresa and a pope and a Beatle. You will eat oranges under the Eiffel Tower, step on the cobblestones of Pompeii, swim under a waterfall in Hawai'i, and straddle two continents while sailing in Istanbul. You will cofound a very successful business. You will sign book contracts for the novels you will write.

But much more important, you will find genuine love with a man who treasures you. You will delight in four children who will bring you immeasurable fulfillment. You will have friends who outnumber the stars. And you will discover that every sorrow and joy is part of a plan for your life by a power higher than yourself. A plan that has meaning and purpose shaped by its highs and lows if you only keep faith as everything unfolds.

You will be given a platform to encourage and inspire others to overcome their difficulties.

Because that's what it's all for. None of it is about you. You are an instrument. You can choose to play sour notes of negativity and self-pity that will compose a cacophonous dirge. Or you can choose to play sweet notes of love and the robust notes of determination that will draw people to something good, something eternal. And in that eternity, you will find a joy beyond your comprehension and an absence of all pain.

Until then, chin up, shoulders back, use sunscreen, lay off the Diet Pepsi, and wash your face every night. Forty is closer than you think, and it will thank you.

*Camille Di Maio lives in Virginia with her husband and four children. She recently left an award-winning career in real estate to become a full-time writer. She's traveled to four continents and most of the states, and she is always planning her next trip.*

51

*Camille loves belting out Broadway tunes at a moment's notice, shopping at farmers' markets, and trying anything that doesn't involve heights or roller skates.*

*She writes historical fiction, and her bestselling novels include The Memory of Us, Before the Rain Falls, and The Way of Beauty.*

# Kimberly Derting

When I asked author Kim Derting to share a love letter to her younger self, she was one of many who found that the words she expected to hit paper were not the ones that found their way onto the page. The sheer love she reflects for her relationship with her mother was a gorgeous surprise as she shared her own advice to her younger self.

Dear Young(er) Kim,

Believe in yourself.

Cliché, I know.

But your mom is right; you're tougher than you think. Smarter too. You're just as good as those who happen to have been born with more—more money, more chances for a better education, those whose families have their you-know-what together.

You just have to hang in there. Keep your nose to the grindstone and all those other hokey sayings. Good things are coming; you just have to work your ass off.

I spend a lot of time thinking about the woman I've become in contrast to where I came from. I know that much of what I've accomplished is because of my determination. But I also have to give credit to the woman who always said I could do it, and here's the thing, young Kim—you should too.

I know you don't believe it now, but you should love your mom more. Hug her. Don't roll your eyes (too often), and try not to be so embarrassed of her. I get how hard that is when literally everything embarrasses you—frizzy hair, the tiniest zit known to humanity, food stuck between your teeth—but get over yourself.

Seriously, your mom's your biggest cheerleader.

Trust me, that woman's got your back, girl. And that will never change.

She'll be there when you get your period, go through your first heartbreak, and tell her you're pregnant at only eighteen. And get this—she'll be excited about it. She'll walk you through stretch marks and hold your hand while you push that screaming, seven-pound, thirteen-ounce little girl into this world.

She'll be your best friend when you get divorced and again when you meet your soul mate and have two more babies. She'll laugh and cry with you, and she'll grow old on you. All the while, you'll learn that you never would have become the woman you are today—living a life you never could have imagined as you were stuck in project housing and standing in the free-lunch line at school.

You were a big dreamer, my friend, but she was always there chanting, "You can do it! I believe in you!"

I'm crying as I write this because I wish I could go back and hug that mom—the one I never appreciated enough. The one I criticized and yelled at. The one I told to drop me off around the corner because I didn't want to be seen with her. I wish I'd told her then what an amazing mother she was and that her faith in me was molding me into a strong, self-sufficient, confident woman.

I tell her now, as often as I can.

I wish you would too.

Love,


Older, no, More Mature Kim

*Kimberly Derting is the author of the award-winning The Body Finder series, The Pledge and The Taking trilogies, and her new contemporary romance, Undressed (The Men of West Beach). Her books have been translated into fifteen languages, and The Body Finder and The Pledge were named YALSA Best Fiction for Young Adults selections.*

*She's fortunate enough to be married to her best friend, and they've raised three amazing children together. She spends her days watching way too much TV and ordering twenty-pound boxes of Nerds gumballs off the internet. She loves to complain about the rain even though she lives in Seattle, where it rains all the time.*

— CHAPTER 7 —

# Writing Your
## ⬦—LOVE LETTER →
# Getting Started

**Y**ou have to love yourself. First. Foremost. Always. Granted, that's easier to read than practice. I'm not talking self-care. Self-care is now almost medically approved. Many studies have shown the correlation between self-care in all its iterations and life happiness, longevity, and the avoidance of disease.

One of the most loving things you can do for yourself is dig in, do the work, learn who you are under all the layers you've put on, and start to love yourself some you. Release all the stories you've been told, and in that painful but blissful work, you will begin to see the you your children and lover see.

Let's get to it.

The rules are simple: trust yourself and harness the tone of a big sister wisely guiding a child. That child just happens to be you, and you know what this young, innocent life will experience. You will be surprised at what you uncover when you approach your younger self with a gentle tone and the wisdom you've attained since you were that girl.

**Do the Work**
**Visualizing Your Younger Self**

Close your eyes and imagine a younger version of yourself. Is she five? Eight? A teenager? See her clearly. What's she wearing? What does her face look like? Is she happy or sad? What emotions do you relate to this image of your younger self?

- Write.

- Write about her clothes, her posture, her face, her image.

- What do you feel when you see her?

- Is there anything she wants from you?

- Now that you have a powerful image of your younger self, trust your gut.

- What do you want her to know?

- The first thing you think is the right thing.

- Write it down.

When I began this exercise, I was blown away by my first sentence. I had an overwhelming desire to tell this dejected little girl I imagined that she was so loved, so worthy. That first sentence hit me like a ton of bricks—"You will spend most of your life believing you are unlovable." I had to take a deep breath and sit back for a moment. I was shocked at how true that sentence was and how it had bled itself into so much of my life and so many of my relationships.

You may feel the same, so give yourself this moment. Just don't leave it because the feelings are too heavy. If you have to wait until the kids are in bed and you have your glass of wine and a box of Kleenex, do that.

Give yourself the gift of time to feel your feelings.

If that means you write one sentence and have to process it for several days before you get back to it, you're still on the path. I have found that most women need time because unlocking these truths has a whiplash effect. They bring up memories and misgivings that no children should believe about themselves.

If you begin unlocking repressed memories or find yourself reeling or having dark thoughts about what you begin to feel, please seek the counsel of a professional therapist.

I've found that the ages the women who have completed these exercises choose are typically aligned with the moment right before or during a tragic or painful event or memory. Just as Chelli wrote to her four-year-old self who was suddenly experiencing abuse at the hands of her uncle, I originally imagined myself at age five, when my mother began drinking and it was clear there were violent things happening in my little world.

You will also notice that your tone changes. The harshness with which you likely view yourself today—*Get it together, sister*—falls away and is replaced with *It's not your fault* or *You're perfect the way you are, love*. You will begin to guide your younger self with the tone of an older sister. Jessica Moore suggested that if we can be gentle with ourselves today, how much healthier we would be.

**Do the Work**
**Going Deeper**

Once you imagine that younger version of yourself and start with the first sentence of your letter, consider the distance between that version of yourself and who you are today. When I'm leading Love Letters workshops, I typically ask women to pull their stories, traumas, and messaging out of them and hold them in their hands as they bubble up. To become separate from them. To think of them as little glass balls each with its own moment, time stamp, or classification much like the memories in the Pixar movie Inside Out. Each memory is infused with whatever corresponding feeling presided over it.

Do this. Let them roll around in your fingers and speak to you. You will begin to see patterns, events, and you won't want to tuck those glass orbs back into your being until you've processed them, cleaned them, and reprogrammed them to sparkle a little brighter.

- How did that first message I shared with my younger self play out over the course of my life? Do I want to carry it with me as I move forward?

- What's one thing I've always known about myself? My greatest strength?

- What's one negative thing I've always known about myself? How was it originally triggered? Was it reinforced by my family? Is it true?

- What's the best thing that has ever happened to me?

- What was my most humbling experience, and what was the lesson?

- What was I missing as a child?

- Whom or what do I need to forgive? Is that person me?

Put your writings away. Let them sit in a safe space for a few days, and then go back to them with a clear mind. Ask yourself how your answers influenced who you are today, what you think about yourself, and how it all affects your relationships with others.

— CHAPTER 8 —

**Tap into Your Subconscious and Find the Story Within**

The act of writing your letter and referring to it will help excavate old programming, memories, and feelings you'd like to release. It will offer you a chance to start fresh at a new point in your growth.

But it is hard. Really hard. Adrianne Haslet and Caroline Heldman took an extended amount of time on their letters, and as I write this chapter, mine is still incomplete. Chelli rewrote hers at least twenty-seven times. You will face ghosts and old memories, but the fact that you might try to avoid them or delay their release just shows you the power they still claim over you.

We have to get to a place of resolution to unlock those stories and be willing to let them seep from our bodies. We have to decide that we want to reclaim our power and keep them from influencing our future decisions, relationships, and imbedded dramas. We have to choose ourselves.

The best way we can find our way in is to put pen to paper or fingers to keys. The act of physically writing is cathartic. Adrianne Haslet, a survivor of the Boston Marathon bombing, shared that there was something about physically moving pen over paper that created a sense of release. There's no wrong way. If you need time to process your truths and stories that have begun to find their way to the surface, begin a free-writing practice. I cannot express enough how important this has been in my life. It's the tool to unlocking your subconscious.

Many times, the first words of my entries are "Fuzzy" or "My mind is scattered." But I keep writing until I work out the kinks, find out what's just beneath the noise and what's right under my swirling thoughts, but it's never perfect.

My entries would be nonsensical to others. The first time I began the Morning Pages suggested in The Artist's Way, my first lines were, "I need Tide. I am out of toothpaste. My closet is a mess. I don't want to do this anymore." I was startled. *What don't I want to do anymore?* But I kept going, and several paragraphs in, I realized how unhappy I was in my current job. I hadn't consciously recognized that I was no longer challenged and was simply complacent. It was a good job. I liked everyone. But I was bored out of my mind. However, my conscious mind had no idea of that.

Later, as my practice progressed, I also realized themes involving my self-worth and what I wanted to manifest in relationships that I hadn't consciously made efforts to correct.

In short, just do it. It works. And when you do, write hard. Write until you have no more words. Then walk away, come back, and write some more. You will eventually find your themes. And they will make their way into your letter and result in big shifts in your life.

— CHAPTER 9 —

*Write hard and clear about what hurts the most.*
*—Ernest Hemingway*

I recently spoke at Kaia Fit's annual retreat in Belize. There was a beautiful woman with glowing skin, shiny hair, big eyes, and a big No. We began our love-letters practice, and as we got to a section where we visualized our future selves, she wasn't interested and said so. Her daughter was a high school student, and she didn't think it would be helpful to visualize because things were going to be so different. "This isn't helpful for me."

She was resisting.

I quietly and respectfully suggested that she consider why she was uncomfortable thinking about the future. Her future. She shared that she had started a business with her husband many years ago that was very successful, but her life revolved around her daughter.

Over the course of the next few days, we discussed what all that meant. Her identity had become Mom, and she would have to shift back to wife and self. Was she ready? She winced and agreed that she wasn't. Deep down, she worried about how it would feel to be alone with her husband again. They would have to remake their relationship as empty nesters.

Another woman spoke up during the same workshop: "I don't want to talk about the past. It's the past. Are we going to dig more into the future? That's the good stuff." I agreed that we were but that we needed to get everyone up to speed.

At the close of the retreat, we had a very honest moment when she said she didn't want to think about the past because that meant she'd have to forgive her mom. She referred to it as releasing the Kraken. If you describe your mother as a legendary sea monster, I suggest that's a lot to walk around with in the vein of comfort.

If you find yourself annoyed by this book—annoyed by me and the stories and angry in any way, shape, or form—consider that you have been triggered. You would totally love me if I wasn't making you do hard stuff.

This happened to me with a woman named Jess, a life coach of sorts who specializes in working with women who have experienced trauma in romantic relationships. Jess is lovely. She's pure light. She also drives me crazy. I can't stand her. At all. It is truly nonsensical. I have no reason not to like her. As the universe would have it, we ran into one another on three occasions through mutual friends we didn't know we shared. The third time, Jess said, "Let's grab lunch." I agreed because it was clear we were supposed to know one another, and I'm always on the hunt for a little universal magic.

We sat in an all-organic cafe in Las Vegas, and she talked about what she did and how she helped women. I was so physically uncomfortable that I wanted to leave. I was angry. I couldn't sit still. I wanted to get away from her as fast as possible. She made me so mad, but I couldn't tell you why. When I told her, "You've triggered me," she asked why, and I started crying big, stupid tears I can't explain. All the issues surrounding relationships that had hurt me to my core came spilling onto a pine table in the suburbs. I hired her as my coach on the spot.

Working with Jess was painful. She had me in places I didn't want to go. I dreaded every session, and I finally told her, "I'm so uncomfortable that I've promised myself I'll keep saying yes. Clearly, there's stuff I need to deal with, and you are bringing it up for me."

We did the work. It was hard. I had to work on issues with my mother, abusive relationships, and experiences I'd preferred to have blocked out and forgotten for the sake of comfort. I had to accept that my coping mechanisms were in the way and learn how to greet these experiences from a healthier place. I hated every second of it. I hated everything about Jess. I hated her voice, the way she talked to me. I hated her holding me to the fire and even supporting me. I'm also glad I did it. I am in a much better place for it, and it sucked.

This may really suck. Lean into your discomfort. If you notice you are uncomfortable, fidgety, angry, sad—then do it. Today. Tomorrow. Whenever. Just do the work. Resolve to excavate the stories that have a stranglehold on you so you can live your best life. Don't be afraid to use this as a catalyst for further help. Work on it with a therapist, a psychologist, a healer. Tell them you have been triggered and start to ask yourself why with the appropriate support in place to help you through it.

## CHAPTER 10

T he women who have done the deepest work took the longest to complete and perfect their letters. It wasn't necessarily because their letters had to be read by others; it was that as they wrote, they found the lighter advice and cute anecdotes suddenly gave way to the darker things they'd buried. They'd often separated themselves from the deeper work through their compensating stories. For some, it was sexual abuse, depression, body issues, or family shame. More than one letter was promised in less than a week, but I would get humble calls or emails that explained they were doing the work, "But can you give me some more time?"

Take your time.

I urge you not to avoid or put it off just because it's painful. Lean into the pain. Allow it to transform from dark to light through your free-writing. Eventually, a sentence or two will come to you with profound clarity. Once your subconscious is done processing the details, it will deliver these gems as if they were the utterances of your soul.

Some writers keep the letters close to refer to over time. One keeps hers next to her bed to remind herself how far she's come and reflect on the caring tone she had for her younger self. Many women have found it cathartic to share their letters with friends and loved ones. If you feel it would be helpful for others, please share your findings. You may also submit it to this project at www.loreandlittlethings.com. We curate and publish select letters from readers for viral mentorship and growth.

PART TWO

the Present //

CHOOSE

*Everything in your life is a reflection of a choice you made. If
you want different results, start making different choices.*
—Dr. Wayne Dyer

The women I've interviewed for this project are beautiful blends of soft and hard, of strength and grace. They also hold your feet to the flame of self-awareness. There is no complaining about their lot in life, about their hardships. They have stories, tragedies, and events that could have been their ending, but each had an internal mettle and the awareness that they had choices.

They didn't expect anyone else to live their lives for them, to take away their right to opportunities or happiness. Each woman chose to rise above what may have taken out another. My friends have often asked me how I was able to look at the past and my relationship with my mother with a healthy perspective. I simply answered, "I've been away from her longer than I was with her. It's on me now."

My executive coach refers to this as the right to harm versus the right to choose. He suggests that we have the ability to move from a place of reaction, an ego-based orientation, to one of creation where all is possible. Oprah Winfrey calls the right to choose your own path "a sacred privilege." The question then becomes, do you own your power? Do you choose to choose?

You are the maker of your life. It's not the responsibility of others to unwind their poor words, parenting, or actions to free you. It's on you now. You must unhook yourself from their influence and the stories you have told yourself and become your own best advocate.

If you want a better, more fulfilling life, you have to take responsibility for it and move from a place of story to a place of action. Are you operating from a place of passivity and awaiting the answers, a savior, or a sign, or have you moved to one of action? Your personal power can be wielded only by you, but you have to choose it and the alchemy it offers.

I have always approached choices from my deathbed. Maudlin maybe, but it's effective. Each time I face fear, malaise, or a big decision, I imagine this woman, this future me. She lies in a bed surrounded by loved ones. Death is imminent. She's looking at me and wondering why I had waited around and hadn't taken action. I shared this with a friend, and she responded, "Oh God!" that smacked of macabre and concern. I'm grateful for the old lady.

Now, she looks at me, who feigns aches and expenses, with a sort of disdain. Do I want to take the risk? Do I want to save up for the thing that seems unattainable? The thing that seems so far away now but the thing the deathbed me will wish I'd done? *Live, girl.* That's right. She talks to me. She sits up in bed and tells me her ride better not be boring because if she's dealing with Medicaid and tearful eyes— (Picture her gesturing to all the miserable people offering well wishes and thinking *Seriously? This shit is depressing*)—she wants to assure them that they shouldn't be sad because she's lived a full life and is heading on to her next adventure with no regrets.

We often worry about the time or expense accomplishments and experiences will require. I live by the adage, "The time will pass anyway."

**Do the Work**
**Deathbed Wishes**

It's your last day on this earth and you are making peace with it.

- What would you wish you had accomplished?

- What experiences do you wish you hadn't missed?

- What is your biggest regret? Whom do you wish you would have shown more love to?

- Is there anything that seems onerous, expensive, or time consuming that you would regret not doing during your lifetime?

- When you look at the foot of your bed, at your loved ones, imagine their eyes.

- Is there anything that should be forgiven now?

- What choices have you made recently that could be unwound or reconfigured to move you closer to the future self you imagine?

- Knowing that this day would come, what different choices would you start making tomorrow?

- Write them down. Today.

- Start with the fundamentals.

- Who surrounds you?

- Who influences you?

- Who is in your ear and taking up space in your head?

- Whom do you spend your time with? Do they cheer for you when you achieve?

- How are you showing up in life?

- Do you believe in your value and worthiness?

- What choices are you making to better yourself?

- Who are your role models?

- Who are your influencers?

You have the power to build your life, your team, your relationships. Don't wait until you're looking wistfully or regretfully back at your life. Start with the most important person first—you.

## CHAPTER 12

# THE GUT-CHECK Method

All the answers are in you. You just have to learn to listen. Some call it women's intuition; others call it your gut. Children and dogs have it down, but sometime during our lives as we are being told how to behave in social settings and are being conditioned by others, we begin to question our innate knowingness and move further away from it.

My knowingness showed up like a displaced relative shortly after my divorce, and I couldn't get it to go away. It's as if I'd had it set to "ignore" until it was time for me to navigate the world as a single mother. Now, I trust it implicitly but only because it has served me well time and again.

Perhaps the best way to befriend your gut, heart, or intuition—whatever word is best for you—is to learn how to listen to your body. When an overbearing relative calls you, how does your body respond? When you face people who are giving you kind smiles but something about them raises the hairs on your arms, what do you do? When you are with someone and you find yourself crossing your arms protectively in front of yourself, do you notice that?

A little over a year ago, I was chatting with a woman who asked if she could see my ring. It's a rose quartz ring that is symbolic to me for personal reasons. Anyone who's familiar with the meanings of stones understands that rose quartz is protective, and that you're not to allow others to touch it. I didn't want to get into the dirty details of my spirituality or superstitions with this woman I barely knew, so I took it off and handed it to her with the intention of cleansing it that evening.

As she slipped it on her finger, she looked at me knowingly and said, "I just took your power. Any shaman will tell you not to let others touch your stones."

I felt a shift in my body. My guard rose. This woman had intentionally tested me and then "took" my power. I felt a sense of unease and distrust, but that was in reaction to her actions. It was the following event that showed where intuition began to step in.

I shared the story about the ring with a friend I love dearly but with whom I've also had a long history that includes both moments of silence and moments of bliss. After I told her about the ring, she gently placed her fingers on it while we were out at dinner one night. I felt my stomach sink as I simply looked at her. I was curious. Knowing what the other woman had done, why would she do the same? I filed it away, but I was aware.

A week later, she came by my house. As she passed through my bedroom at one point, she deliberately laid her palm on a large rose quartz heart I have on the table next to my bed. I looked at her forcefully and said, "Stop touching my shit!" Then I hissed at her. Like a cat. I don't hiss at people. The fact that this noise or action came out of me immediately signaled my gut check. The whole thing seemed silly—the testing, the guardedness about rocks. I kept trying to pass these trespasses off as such in my mind. They're just things. But I couldn't ignore the fact that she was disrespecting my feelings and testing my resolve. *No, she can't be. She knows how I feel.*

What shook me however was the fact that I had actually hissed at her. My mind was trying to make sense of it, but my body let me know without question that I could argue away all the details but that her actions had been predatory.

We must learn to trust ourselves. We talk ourselves in and out of situations, in and out of conflict. Could we instead learn to scan our bodies for the truth? Rather than arguing away our responses or finding ourselves defensive, could we trust that something makes us feel uncomfortable and allow that to be our answer?

**Do the Work**
**The Gut Check**

From this moment on and for the next week, actively begin to listen to your body as you interact with the world. Learn to trust yourself in a way you may never have consciously before. Pay attention to how you feel as you receive texts, calls, and emails. Do you cringe or steady yourself to open the messages? In interactions with others, do you find your posture changing—your shoulders curling in on yourself—or even assuming a defensive stance as others enter your space?

When someone shares news with you, do you lean into it? Feel uncomfortable? Find yourself questioning? Pay attention to your breathing, your posture, and your instincts as you receive information. Start to track patterns. You don't have to assign full meanings to them; you can simply say, "When I see so-and-so's name appear on my phone, I feel nervous."

- Start there.

- Then ask yourself some questions.

- What does this tell me about this person?

- About myself?

- About the nature and worthiness of our relationship?

## CHAPTER 13

## ACTIVE Orientation

**W**e make choices every day. Some are automatic, ingrained, easy. We shop at the same grocery store, buy the same roasted coffee, mindlessly wrap presents for our children's teachers every year because that's expected, the right thing to do.

Other choices require thought, fortitude, conviction. These choices determine where we go to school, our professions, and how we choose our relationships. Yes, we choose our relationships in all their glory and gunk. The magic is in allowing our choices to be active as opposed to passive or story-based, and that requires significant self-awareness.

Learning to tap into our inner dialogue and achieving self-awareness is the first step in shifting our orientation. We have to consciously notice when we are triggered, become our own observer, and study that soft spot. We can choose to react of course. We all have people who know exactly what buttons to push. When they do and we suddenly want to scream, cry, or throw things, we should take a moment, pause, and ask ourselves what they have triggered in us.

We must choose to take notice and study ourselves. We have to learn to move from the vulnerable place of feeling the feeling and its external emotional response to the place of noticing it. *What is this right here? Yes, I see you. You smell like fear, abandonment issues, unworthiness. Hi, friend.*

My executive coach once told me the story of Siddhartha Gautama, who became Buddha, and the demon, Mara. Mara continually tried to pull Siddhartha from his path to enlightenment by acting as his serpent of sorts. Again and again he offered him distractions—lust, greed, anger, and doubt. Siddhartha remained firm and became enlightened. Mara persisted, but instead of driving him away or ignoring him, the Buddha would calmly acknowledge him. "I see you, Mara." He then invited him for tea as an honored guest and offered him comfort and hospitality.

Invite your fear and pain for tea. Learn to see them. Granted, at times, it's hard to figure out how you feel about something, just that it's off, uncomfortable. You go into a static mind-set or what feels more like mind-rest and allow things to swirl and happen around you without moving to active orientation. You process and feel things you can't quite name. You begin making passive choices with your inaction.

You should lean into those moments. Notice the inaction, the passive stance. Start by recognizing there is a feeling swirling around your subconscious and ask yourself what it's there to teach you. As you become consciously aware of your own hesitance, pain, fear, and inner workings, smile at it and say, "I see you, Mara. Come have tea." After dining with your demon, you will find a more direct path to action. The act of noticing and accepting creates a path toward active-choice orientation.

**Do the Work**
**Active-Choice Orientation**

Spend a few minutes considering the decisions you wish you would've made differently.

- How did choice play into your decision-making? Were you active or passive?

- Think of the best decisions you've made. How were they different? What choices are you currently considering?

- Spend a few minutes trying to find your Mara. What feelings are attached to the decision? How can you make a move from passive to active? What information would you need to take that leap?

— CHAPTER 14 —

*Choice*
AND
*Self Worth*

> *There is no greater power*
> *than that of the sun,*
> *the moon, and a woman*
> *who knows her worth.*
> *-Nicole Lyons*

**W**hen you value yourself less, you tend to put up with things you shouldn't. Knowing your worth or value is the cornerstone of how the world will respond to you. It creates the map on which all else falls into place. Your relationships in all their iterations—friendships, coworkers, family, or romantic relationships—are navigated by the guidance you provide. Your value, the choice you make about your health, happiness, and self-respect, creates the North Star of your relationships.

At times, you remain tied to old acquaintances, complicated long-term relationships, places, and memories. You may find it hard to choose yourself over shared history or the way things are. The tangles and webs of familial stories are hard to unravel, yet I guarantee that if you begin to see yourself as a person of worth and value, they will slowly fall into line. Or be pushed into line. Or shoved.

You may hear a lot of "You've changed," but that should make you smile. You've simply moved from a place of acceptance when offered less than you deserve to one of value. Others may test the waters and create uncomfortable conversations and confrontations. That is an opportunity to set expectations about what you value in your relationships. Over time, even those who are hesitant to accept the new you will get used to your redrawn boundaries.

Relationships can be redirected to work for all involved, but if a little redirection doesn't work, you will have to have the strength to call it. This is more difficult in long-term and romantic relationships, but as you learn your value and choose yourself, you will know who is worth working with and who needs to be allowed to find his or her way out of your life.

Concentrate on you, your values, and don't become disheartened if more people leave than stay. As you grow your worth, you will raise the standards by which you operate and of what you tolerate. Less fighting. More harmony. You begin making room for people who truly value you. It's a win-win though there are growing pains in the interim.

I recently ended a twelve-year friendship very unceremoniously. I wanted to believe there was love there, history. *Of course we can get through our differences.* But when patterns became clear and I realized I'd been lied to and manipulated, it was very simple. I don't make room for liars in my life. I remember the words coming to me as if I'd known them in my soul so completely so many years before they found their way out of my mouth—"I'm done."

That night started a soulful cleanup of my crew and a very specific line in the sand for future romantic relationships. I realized I didn't want anyone in my life who made me feel bad, asked me why I was wearing a certain outfit or why my brows were unwaxed, or made me feel guilty in any way.

If you made me question myself in a way that was unloving, you were out. I had unwittingly just taken a master class in manipulation and could sniff you out before honey dripped from your lips. If you talked trash about other people in your life, I knew you wouldn't hesitate to do the same with me. If I was happy about something and you couldn't be happy for me, I knew that was about you and it wouldn't change. I knew I'd have to mute myself, but I would never press mute again. If my posture changed when you reached out to me, I knew you weren't good for me. I had to choose me. So I did. Unapologetically. Over and over.

In the process, I stumbled upon some of the strongest, most present people I've ever met, many whose letters and insights grace this book. One of them is Jessica Moore. She wrote in her letter about her deep relationships with women, and in the resulting interview, we discussed those she held close. She shared that she recognized the influence her relationships had over her and her influence over them. She chooses them wisely because of this, and it is her personal thought that we should leave people better than we found them, enriching their lives.

I met actress, activist and supermodel Patricia Velasquez in Sun Valley, Idaho, last year when we were asked to participate in The Alturas Institute's "Conversations With Exceptional Women." I absolutely adored her take on friendships. She explained that she has a gluten allergy and realized when she avoided gluten, her body felt significantly better and more healthy. As she was listening in to her body, she also began to realize that some relationships made her feel badly: "I realized some people are gluten. There's nothing necessarily 'wrong' with them. I just have to avoid them because to me they are gluten."

Fox Sports reporter Jamie Little wrote of the need to keep your circle tight and "trim the fat." It sounds daunting, this deselection of relationships, but it doesn't have to be. So many times, we let history and guilt keep us around people we've either outgrown or who bring us back to places we've left. We make excuses for others' bad behavior— "That's just so-and-so God love her (or him)." I agree God does love her. But if so-and-so is not growing with you, is keeping you down, hurting you, mistreating you, consider loving her from afar. Send her love and light. If you need permission to say goodbye, here I am. I give you permission. Not everyone is meant for the long haul. Thank her for whom she has been to you.

Then choose you.

Choosing yourself does not require writing an epithet on all the sins of another. It doesn't have to be the breakup heard around the world. I wouldn't recommend you send out a Facebook announcement, "If you can see this message, congratulations—I didn't unfriend you" followed by a diatribe about how it was time to clean house. Simply decline invitations. Fill your calendar and your soul with people and activities that spur you to a better version of yourself.

If the relationship in question is more complicated, maybe that with a spouse or partner, consider counseling to realign the values of your relationship. As a recovering, hopeless romantic, I want all couples to work out if possible. I believe wholeheartedly in trying, reminding one another why you originally chose to be together, and reestablishing boundaries, commitments, and intimacy.

Can you choose one another again? One of my closest friends told me she chooses her husband every morning. She believes true love includes a hell of a lot of choices when the spark fizzles or times are tough. But there are times when trying doesn't, won't, or shouldn't work, and it's more important to choose yourself. You will know.

Another friend recently left her husband. She was struggling with her feelings of having been unhappy for many years. He questioned her abilities as a mom and a wife regularly and resented her for a variety of reasons. She was beating herself up with guilt, but she couldn't take the way he made her feel any longer. She was sick with indecision and grief. I offered that if she didn't know, then maybe wait until she did—coparent, talk to friends, get quiet with herself, journal, figure out how she felt away from his disheartening words. I told her one day she may just wake up and know.

Three months later, she called me and said, "I woke up this morning and I knew. It hit me so clearly. I don't want to be married to him any longer." She chose herself.

After I chose myself in my many friendships, several of my old friends (and a few exes I decided to distance myself from) reached out. Without blame or judgment, I answered their questions about my silence. I honestly told one woman that whenever we had been together, she had told me my accomplishments made her feel lazy and bad about herself. I told her that her words had made me uncomfortable. I didn't want to spend time with someone who required I edit my happiness. I told her that if she felt those things, maybe they were her own self-talk. "I can't make you feel anything," I said.

I told an ex that I didn't appreciate the reminiscent way he would reach out and eventually bring up the flaws of our past relationship. I knew it was manipulative; I'd allowed it for too long. I'd sigh or roll my eyes whenever his name popped up on my phone.

I created a very specific boundary for each relationship I ended or held at arm's length. Oddly, every one of the people I had a hard conversation with was understanding. They recognized they were unhappy or facing their own difficulties. A few asked me what they could do to help improve their own feelings of inadequacy and low self-esteem. I suggested books, journaling, meditation, and lots of self-love.

The act of standing up for and bettering myself gave my friends the permission they needed to do the same. It turned out to be just what they needed to reset and look within before we reached out to each other again.

**Do the Work**
**Choose Yourself**

Here are questions to ask yourself to determine which relationships require a bit of restructuring or a whole lot of boundaries.

- Are they happy for me when I achieve?

- Do I groan or wince when their names show up on my phone?

- Do I find myself changing aspects of my personality or the way I present myself around this person?

- Do interactions with certain people leave me feeling drained, tired, or negative, or am I happy and uplifted from having engaged with them?

- Do I feel safe with them?

- Do I trust them?

- Would I want them to spend time with my children without me?

- Do they talk negatively about other people?

- Do I worry they talk negatively about me?

- Do I feel the need to gossip or be negative to engage with them?

— CHAPTER 15 —

The Relationships
WE CHOOSE

**W**hen we compare our innate desire to be loved and attain those things modeled in Cinderella stories against the shock of real life, it is startling. I don't have many women writing letters about their wonderful relationships. Most of the women I've interviewed or surveyed have flawed histories with men. They have done deep, internal work. It is a spiritual belief that our greatest proving ground and opportunity for growth is in our relationships. The letters and interviews confirm this without question.

Past failed relationships and rebuilt marriages after infidelity or addiction are what have created the healthy relationships women now have or aspire to. This is the work they wish they could share with their younger selves. As serendipity would have it, it all leads back to choice.

For better or worse, we choose the relationships we enter. I used to be completely annoyed by the expression, "Every woman has the love life she wants." Someone threw it at me as if it were a challenge while I was in the depths of a formidable breakup. I couldn't understand how it was possible to choose all the pain I was experiencing.

In hindsight, I realized I'd brought it all on myself. My lack of self-esteem and my desire to be seen and loved caused me to choose men who were, to put it plainly, unworthy of me. They may have pursued me, but even when red flags waved, I chose to ignore them. Instead, I chose them back. I chose their red flags and all the eventual pain. *This time will be different. He won't do that to me. He's changed.*

You'll often hear people say they married their mothers or their fathers; their lovers were exact replications of others who had modeled their understanding of how to give and receive love. Others have shared that familial belief systems about gender had influenced how they approached their love lives.

I asked women about the partners they had chosen and was blown away by one writer's response: "I didn't select men. They selected me." She explained that she had a very low opinion of herself and that broken men had sought her out. Brandi cried more than she laughed. She believed that love was supposed to hurt. She thought she could fix them, but over time, she became their punching bag.

Brandi had been molested at age nine by her uncle. Her family had very antiquated views on a woman's place in the home, and though the women in her family were strong, one was heard telling her daughter on her wedding night, "Just let him do what he wants. It's your duty as his wife."

When her uncle's marriage failed, the family said it was because her aunt hadn't tried harder. Brandi's nine-year-old mind blamed the abuse she experienced on her aunt's inability to please her uncle. She became sexually active at a very young age and dated anyone who showed her attention. Out of desperation for love, she sacrificed mind, body, and soul but received very little in return.

She is now in a respectful, loving relationship but only after making very specific choices about what she would allow in her life. She excavated her old understanding of worth: "Love feels good, not desperate. It feels safe, not suspicious. Trust your gut."

Chelli Wolford spoke of her belief that she could love a broken man "better." She felt her love was so powerful that she could love the pain out of another. In her interview, she spoke of the realization that domestic violence was becoming an undercurrent in her relationships and she was done. Done. She had to choose herself and engage in the very hard work that comes along with self-discovery if she wanted to blow up her old way of choosing men. In the past, she had felt she wasn't worthy of a good guy because she was too broken. She had to reprogram herself to realize she was absolutely deserving of a good guy whom she jokingly also referred to as "boring."

We talked about that hard work, and she shook her head. "What's worse? Being uncomfortable and in pain because you're healing, or continuing these terrible cycles? The work, at least, has a happy ending. My relationships did not."

I chose men who hated themselves. I hand-selected very handsome, charming narcissists on far too many occasions only to fall into utter heartbreak and confusion when the blackness inside them unleashed itself on me.

One such man kept me up late into the night as he was in a drunken stupor; he shared everything he hated about me. He hated the sound of my voice, the shape of my teeth, and my "mouse eyes." To watch and listen to a person you are in love with unleashing their deep insecurities and self-hatred on you is devastating. It took me back to days my mother would do the same—sit on the end of my bed drunk, wake me in the middle of the night, and list my transgressions. That triggered the same question: How can anyone who professes love for me hurt me like this?

I had chosen someone who loved me like my mother did when she was at her worst. When I finally realized the correlation between my childhood understanding of love and the patterns I remained in, I made a list of all the things I wanted to see and feel in my relationships. I got specific with myself and learned the values that were important to me. This exercise works to reprogram your "picker." It helps you understand the characteristics and qualities you've unconsciously sought out and select those who become the bedrocks of stronger partnerships.

Whether you are single or married, take the time to list the values and characteristics important for you in relationships. It is also important to consider what qualities you bring to the table. What does your partner appreciate most about you? What values could you better emulate? Creating this purposeful dialogue whether internally or with your partner about your relationship will give you the opportunity to build it from stone as opposed to simply be sheltered inside it waiting for the storm.

After all, every woman has the love life she wants.

**Do the Work**
**Reflection Point**

Consider your past relationships.

- How is your "picker?"

- Do you notice patterns?

- Have those same patterns appeared in your existing relationships?

- What have the partners you've chosen had in common?

- Have any of them reminded you of messaging from your parents?

Write down the values and attributes that are most important to you in a relationship and what you bring to the table.
Ask yourself if you have chosen life partners who reflect the values and attributes you find most important. Did you show up as your best self?

Free-write your answers and the reasons you made the choices you did in those experiences.

## CHAPTER 16

*Choose the man who wipes away your tears instead of the one who
makes you cry. Choose brains over beauty and a sense of humor over
almost anything else. (And don't choose any man at all until you're
happy with the woman you see when you look in the mirror.)*
—*Jessica Moore*

L oving yourself first and realizing how amazing you are immediately
sets the tone for self-respect, the magic ingredient when modeling to
others how you should be treated. You may think you do a great job of
loving and respecting yourself. You go to the gym, you journal—hell,
you may even be in yoga teacher training.

All important, but I appreciate what Jessica said to help get single
women there a little faster. She advised women to live alone before they
commit to live with another. Even better if a woman lives alone while
remaining single. That is when she finds out who she is and what it
means to love herself.

Jessica argued that you find out what you are made of, your
strengths, and your capacity to survive and inspire yourself. You should

become a woman of capability before assigning yourself to the age-old ideal of attaching yourself to a man to do the "hard" things. Women can do very hard things. After you dispose of a dead rat that made the unfortunate decision to enter your house via the dog door (fun chew toy for pets), kill a scorpion under your stiletto while juggling bags, fish a deceased bird out of a pool, and take care of yourself (and your child) while you're sick or recovering from outpatient surgery, you will realize that you are your own person without another. When he arrives, you will appreciate him and yourself more than you can imagine.

Loving yourself first is not simply for the single woman. It is also for you, Mama. I see you. The one with the husband, the kids, and the Starbucks addiction who reads the last paragraph wishing she could go lease an apartment to live alone. Oh my God! What is quiet? The one who hustles between work and family responsibilities trying really hard to eat and clean and who winces when she feeds her kid McDonald's. *Just this once.*

You may relate to Sarah Jessica Parker in I Don't Know How She Does It. She's my spirit animal. Yes, you. You have to love yourself first, and as I've said so many times, self-care, self-love, is the most selfless thing there is. You have nothing to give others if you don't love yourself first.

I asked women how they do this when they've been married for some time. How do they learn to love themselves first when they are on anniversary number twelve and kid number two needs to be in cleats and on the field in twenty?

Most of the women I interviewed shared that they and their husbands express their needs and act in partnership with one another. They respect each other's aspirations, and what fills each tank is different. This allows for separate interests, recognition of stressors, and more often than not, more communication and closeness. When you voice your needs and offer space for your spouse to do the same, you create understanding and intimacy.

April shared that carving out alone time for herself was actually a message to her children that marriage did not mean you had to dedicate your life to someone else's happiness. Her husband loves to sit on the beach for hours at a time, but she doesn't. So when they are in an RV for a week or two at a time, she may read a book inside or use the car to go into town while he sits by the ocean. He doesn't feel abandoned by her or as if she doesn't want to participate because she's made her feelings known. April doesn't feel as if she needs to pressure him to leave his precious beach time to explore shops and museums. They come together for the things they both enjoy.

We are responsible for our own happiness or peace; we cannot do that for others. Fill your own soul, but also understand what fills the soul of the one you love.

**Do the Work**
**Love Yourself First**

How do you love yourself first? Does that question make you laugh? Then write why.

- What calms your spirit?

- What feeds your soul?

- What feeds your partner's soul?

- If you could carve twenty minutes out of every day for just you, what would you do?

## CHAPTER 17

## Appropriate BOUNDARIES

**O**ur boundaries establish what we consider acceptable when it comes to the behavior and interactions of those we walk through life with be they personal or work-related friends. Most of us have work to do in learning how and when to set boundaries, and they are much easier laid when we have a firm understanding of self.

When you know what you are capable of and have enough space between yourself and others, you know what is acceptable. It's when you become enmeshed in relationships, perhaps familial or codependent, that your boundaries blur and it can become more difficult to enact appropriate guidelines for the way you will be treated. There is a very big difference between love and attachment, and while I can't offer you the clinical representations of either, I can tell you that at first, they both feel loving, flattering, and intentional. One offers you space. The other offers you headaches, blurred lines, and more conversations and insecurities than can be covered in one book.

We learn how to create boundaries as children in our homes and our friendships, the testing grounds for what comes with hormones and dreams of weddings and babies. Unfortunately, we also have a tendency to think of children as another species without free will or opinions. As their parents, we often bend their little wills to our ways and remind them they are second class in our homes. I was very fortunate to have a father who always asked himself, Is she testing her voice, or is she being a punk? when I flexed my spindly little muscles. He said he never wanted to break my spirit.

When I asked a group of women if they were allowed to create boundaries as children, whether the ubiquitous no was allowed, or if they were encouraged to form boundaries as they began dating, the majority said one of two things: they were not allowed to have boundaries as children, and romantic or sexual relationships were not discussed.

Most women said there were never conversations about their bodies. They were told, "Cover up" and "Don't be stupid" and left to their own devices. Many times, that led to early premarital sex and great shame. For some, the lack of those conversations manifested itself as inappropriate boundaries that had to be rewritten much later in life. One woman astounded me with her clarity: "I felt as if my body was there to please men. I didn't own it because I'd never been told what to do with it. Just what others wanted to do with it."

Children who do not feel comfortable telling someone how they'd like to be treated grow into adults who are nervous about upsetting another with their concerns. These are women who start sentences with apologies—"I know you've probably thought of this, and I really don't want to be a bitch, but …" Most children with a strong sense of self or clear boundaries are considered by others to be willful or sassy.

A parent may fall into age-old programming that requires children to remain silent, obedient, and under the parent's thumb. A conscious shift of the parent/child dynamic is required to move from one of "What I say goes" or "I'm the boss" to a safe place for children to test their boundary-making abilities.

My mother did not allow boundaries, so my daughter is being raised with the ability to create her own whenever she feels it's appropriate. She recently told me, "Mom, you know how sometimes we call each other crazy when we're being silly? Well, I don't mind you doing that at home, but I don't want you to call me crazy in front of my friends. I get embarrassed." I smiled at the very clear line she had drawn. Some might roll their eyes and argue, "I'm your parent. I'll say what I want," or dismiss their children, but as with all things, I imagine my child in several years. I'm confident she will be able to tell her first boyfriend, "I don't like that. Don't do it," with the same firm tone she used with me. So I nodded my head in agreement and respect for the woman she will become. "I hear you. I won't do that again. Thank you for telling me."

I am thrilled that my daughter has the ability to set the boundaries I wasn't able to; I allowed people to walk all over me as I moved from teenage to adult relationships, platonic and romantic. As I recognized my worth, I was subject to truth bombs that were startling in their delivery and arrival. When I allowed partners to take their arguments too far and suddenly found myself saying in a steely voice I didn't recognize, "Don't come at me like that," or "I don't love that," or "That makes me uncomfortable," I took note of the unknown part of me that had spoken a very big truth. These small words, these verbal shields were saying, "You're crossing my boundaries." Every time I spoke those words and with force, the other parties backed down. If someone returned to the argument when my defenses were lowered, I knew that person had a problem with boundaries.

If you find yourself repeatedly guarding yourself or standing up for yourself in moments of conflict with the same person, it may be time to allow that person to find the boundary of your porch. If someone won't respect your boundaries or tries to argue them away, that person is not good for you. Another imposing his or her viewpoints, beliefs, and feelings on you with no regard for your own will not change. You cannot change someone who does not respect boundaries. You must respect your own.

They can go to therapy and call you when they've had a breakthrough, but any time prior to that, they're off limits. If the offender is a man, please note that it is not romantic to be pursued or challenged when you establish boundaries. His form of love is rooted in disrespect, and when your no stops sounding like a no to him, you're being shown a very big red flag, one that's more like a red parachute. Or a Mack truck.

**Do the Work**
**Boundaries**

- Use the following questions to free-write a paragraph or more about your relationship with boundaries.

- Were you allowed to create boundaries as a child?

- Do you allow your children and loved ones to create boundaries?

- How do you feel when someone enacts a boundary?

- How do you feel when you enact a boundary?

- How do you feel when someone disrespects your boundaries?

- Think of one place where you could set an effective boundary. How would following through on enforcing this boundary make you feel in the long term?

## CHAPTER 18

*Healthy Conflict*
*AND*
*Communication*

Being able to impress upon your partner or your friends and coworkers when you have been aggrieved or hurt is brave and necessary. Many times, the conflicts we are afraid of breed the greatest resentment. As amazing as it would be, most of us are still incapable of reading minds. We allow unspoken hurts to fracture our most sacred relationships all under the guise of comfort.

Conflict is uncomfortable, but so are relationships that are so far gone due to a lack of communication that deep work is required to find one another again. That hurts worse.

Conflict creates understanding and intimacy. Women who have come out of difficult relationships and abusive patterns share that they are no longer fearful of conflict in their relationships. They found their worth, determined what they will and won't accept in relationships, enact strong boundaries, and have chosen partners who respect them. Both parties understand that relationships require work but do not have to be hard. They are not fearful of sharing their concerns or expressing themselves.

One woman, Jessica Leigh, who historically suffered from issues of worth, shared, "I am currently with an incredible man. I feel like I got here because I had to learn how to live with radical vulnerability and very real boundaries that I adhered to. Me first. I listened to my needs. I took care of them. I cared about him and showed it and spoke to it, but I took care of myself first." She and Brandi explained that they respectfully and honestly communicate with their partners. Nothing is off limits.

Brandi, mentioned earlier, said she and her husband recognize that they can debate; they may not always agree, but their mutual love and respect allow them to openly talk and work through issues.

Here's Jessica Leigh's message to other women and girls: "You are worthy of what you want. You are worthy of what you need. There is a huge difference between sacrifice and compromise. You do not have to be scared of conflict. Conflict drives relationships deeper. You want to be with someone who can and shall do the work. Conflict doesn't have to be mean.

"Trust yourself to go deeper. Each partner will help you uncover deeper parts of your heart. You get to say no. You get to say yes. Everyone has lessons, and no one knows. Let go of the results and commit to showing up fully. Stand for your partner to show up fully. Accept nothing less."

Conflict allows deeper intimacy, and many times, it also gives you deeper insight into the things you value most. In From Anger to Intimacy, author Gary Smalley threw a little prayer up each time he and his wife fought; he was thankful for the opportunity to know himself better and love his wife more. He saw it as a bridge to intimacy.

I've often sent friends a list of questions developed by psychologist Arthur Aron to establish a firm foundation of intimacy. I learned of these questions via a *New York Times* article "How to Fall in Love with Anyone" and recently stayed up late with the man I'm dating to dig through the questions convinced it would be fun. After question 19 surrounding "your most terrible memory," I closed my laptop and asked him if he wanted to take a break and make out for a bit. I was thoroughly drained. A few minutes later, we were back at the questions, settled deeper into my couch, and sharing truths that may become the foundation of something great. In the moments I was at my most vulnerable, he met my nervousness with a kiss on my shoulder as I talked.

I've challenged my coupled friends to use these questions as a way to fall back in love with their partners when there is a grievance. To find a way to see that twinkle in their partners' eyes when they talk about high school memories and big dreams. To find them again. To kiss them on their shoulders when they see the humanity and vulnerability of those they may have simply forgotten somewhere between work, the dry cleaner, soccer practice, and Whole Foods.

Author Gary Smalley has also created a list of things he loves about his wife. When they are at their worst, he looks at the long list to remind himself how much he loves her. I completely get that the last thing you want to do is read a list of your husband's shining attributes when you have evicted him from your bed. The ability to refocus on the bigger picture, however, diffuses the initial anger and puts you back to a place of mutual love and respect before you start the "feeling" sentences that go, "When you did (enter bad thing here), I felt …"

My lovely friend, Camille Di Maio, wrote about giving personalities coming together in love—"That's the good stuff." It creates an environment of support and service. How often do you use conflict or intimacy as a reason to reconnect and ask your partner, "Am I helping to make you a better person? How can I serve you?"

Allow yourself to use the words conflict and intimacy with your spouse or partner. Keep them in your mind. Marry them. When you want to run screaming, laugh instead. Look at the sky and thank God for giving you a chance to work on your marriage.

Then you can curse me, but you should be smiling when you do it.

Because karma.

**Do the Work**
**Healthy Conflict and Intimacy**

- What is your relationship with conflict? With intimacy?

- What would you like your partner to know that has been difficult to share or that comes up in arguments regularly?

- How could you use your understanding of your triggers, your Mara, to view the issues from a more distanced position?

- Once you have some perspective, could you find a way to discuss the issues from a place where you desire to create better understanding and intimacy in your relationship?

## CHAPTER 19

*Don't be labeled. Be all things.*
*—Jamie Little*

I adore how themes emerged across letters. The women who faced tragedy shared their own themes primarily having to do with forgiveness and purpose. Those who worked in male-dominated industries wanted women to ask for what they wanted and avoid sexualization or masculinization. Almost every woman regardless of her history said, "Stop caring what people think."

We grow up on the advice and counsel of our parents, our mentors. Some leave the nest and venture into their newly created universes or tribes of friends and coworkers with a stronger sense of self than do others. Some are grounded in who they are, others waffle, but almost all feel the need to prove themselves as they move into new social landscapes.

We wait for feedback from external sources to know that we've assimilated, fit in, achieved. The hope is that at some point, we will understand our gifts and weaknesses and will level out. We feel we've achieved some respect from peers and created a strong group of friends. Unfortunately, many never get to that place; they are constantly in a state of anxiety with a need for approval even with multiple degrees, successful careers, and long-term relationships whether romantic or not.

Dig into your feelings about approval wherever you fit into that spectrum. Understand why you need external approval and if it is healthy or if it is creating unhealthy anxiety. Understand your motivation for approval. If it is career oriented, is it because you want to be seen as capable or receive accolades from leadership and peers? Are you seeking a promotion? A raise? To venture into a new sphere of influence? Or is it ego driven?

As you get close to those you esteem, you will often realize that they don't have the answers either. We're doing the best we can at all times guessing and pontificating based on our stories, education, and experiences. Our thought bubbles are sometimes our only lens.

We are also so many times concerned that someone will learn about our faults or inadequacies that we try hard to shine light on the parts of us that are positive and create compensating stories for our lack. We live in an understated fear of being found out or called a fraud. Many successful people talk about the fraud effect after great achievement. The world may see them as successful, but they sense an undercurrent of unworthiness and old stories that keep them chained to the past and feed a constant yearning for acceptance. There is much catharsis in meeting those old stories and making peace with them.

External approval from our social circle is perhaps where we feel the most vulnerable. These are the people who could hurt us most with their opinions or indifference. Sadly, we never stop to think that they worry about what we think of them as well. We are all trying so hard to be loved by others that we don't stop to love ourselves. That small shift of perception from the external "What do they think?" to the far more important "What do I think?" could move the paradigm.

Finding self-esteem in your internal dialogue and acting from a place of self-respect sets the tone for the way others will value you. You will move from a place of searching for approval to a place of confidence, and your stance will become far more open. People are drawn to your outlook and confidence, and the insecurities begin to fall away. But it starts in you.

**Do the Work**

**Perceptions**

- What decisions have you made based on others' perceptions?

- Consider the basis for the approval of others: Is it based in fact? Is it ego driven?

- What do they think about me?

- What do I think about me?

- What am I afraid for others to know about me? What am I most ashamed of and why?

- Could I meet that shame head-on and learn from it?

- If they really knew me and the things I'm most embarrassed about, what would change?

— CHAPTER 20 —

*Overcoming* SOCIAL *Influence*

I recently gave a talk entitled "Is It True? Challenging the Stories We Tell Our Children." I had taken Olivia's trademark question and dug into it a little deeper. I shared with the audience that while I was deconstructing my messaging and building something new, I was supremely aware I had to take it a step further and create a sense of awareness around messages I was receiving. The resulting realization made me sad and caused me to share with a good friend recently, "I think I'm giving myself body dysmorphia. These Instagram models are nothing but trouble."

While I'd learned not to harp on my thighs or complain that I couldn't lose some stubborn belly fat in front of my daughter, I was blown away by the initial thoughts I'd have when I scrolled through my social media feeds. I thought that following fit moms would make me feel inspired and motivated, but instead, I found myself feeling more insecure than I had ten minutes before.

This little thought bubble kept showing up whenever I'd see someone with a twenty-four-inch waist and a booty, *I wish I looked like that*. Here's the thing: I'm not genetically predisposed to an hourglass shape, so getting that would require a significant change in my daily schedule, be difficult to maintain, and would likely drive me crazy. Yet there I was pining for something that was unattainable. How many of us do that and sometimes without realizing how detrimental it is to our emotional health and the self-image of those impressionable miniature versions of ourselves?

This thought coupled with another experience in Phoenix made me aware of our need to consciously construct our messaging. Entrepreneur Amy Jo Martin mentors a thirteen-year-old girl named Aleena Valdez, who has written a letter to her future self. Aleena is also an entrepreneur and philanthropist who created Girls for Progress, a conference for girls by girls. Amy Jo asked me to speak at the inaugural conference to a roomful of adolescent and teen girls about their future selves, the women they were to become.

I was nervous to speak at Aleena's event more so than I was talking to CEOs and celebrities. I wasn't sure I could connect with these girls. I hadn't been in their headspace for a long time, and we all expect teenagers to be moody creatures. I walked them through a visualization exercise in which I had them imagine what their future self looked like and who surrounded her, her career, and her influence.

I asked for volunteers and saw a hand go up to my left. I walked over to a humble thirteen-year-old girl with long brown hair and a hopeful look. I could see she wanted so badly to connect with someone. She completely floored me with her answer. "My future self will be blond, tall, and confident, the complete opposite of me today." She tilted her head as if apologizing for taking up space. I felt the mama lion in me take over.

I knew in my bones that I had to stand in that space and honor her without embarrassing her in front of her peers. I made a joke about highlights and hair bleach, how I'd grown up blond but my hair had become darker, how we all wanted what we didn't have, how I wore heels to appear taller. I was trying to normalize the deep emotions so I didn't parent her but instead led her to a safe space to consider who she was without the insecurities she had laid bare.

I suggested that rather than asking for height, she ask to be tall in her power, tall in her voice, and tall in her compassion. I said that she would feel six feet tall when she entered a room by those characteristics alone. Then I felt myself ground into the floor knowing I had to leave her with something she'd always remember. "You are already confident. It's already in you, growing. You were the first to raise your hand and share with this room. That's confidence, love. And another thing." She nodded her head waiting. "You're beautiful. You will grow to love things about yourself that today you wish you could change. That I promise you."

She grew about four more inches in that moment, and I realized I would have to think on my feet for the rest of the session offering these girls connection and presence.

These very present young women told me they didn't feel sure they could accomplish things because they were girls. They talked Kardashians and Instagram models. They were trying to understand how they were supposed to be women when they were still carrying around their baby fat. They were girls trying to figure out how to be women in a world that asked them to be sexy, smart, bosses, kind, and competitive, and that was a lot of pressure. I was amazed at their bravery and honesty. I realized that these words were words no one had given them permission to say out loud.

What are we doing to our girls? Ourselves?

I walked them through an exercise in which we talked role models and discussed the difference between those we select and those who surreptitiously select us.

When I sat with Patricia Velasquez in her home in LA to discuss her advice to her younger self, this very topic arose. We discussed her career as a supermodel and her edict that her eleven-year-old daughter, Maya, not have an Instagram account. "Social media is not real," she said. She went on to share that whether or not she was the former face of Cover Girl or graced global fashion magazines, her biggest struggle was with self-esteem and rejection. She advises girls to realize that what they see is curated, not a true interpretation of life, and that most women they see as pinnacles of perfection struggle with deep issues surrounding body image and self-esteem.

**Do the Work**
**Observing Social Influence**

Who is influencing your thoughts daily? Make a list of the information you receive be it gossip with the girls, your social media feed, TV programs, or magazines. Take notice of who is doing the role modeling in your life. Observe the way it makes you feel and what quiet thoughts sneak through your filters.

## CHAPTER 21

Take a look at the messages you receive daily. It's no longer your parents. You forgave them in the last section. External forces are molding and enabling you. Are these people your aspirations or entertainment? Can you zero in on the difference?

The first thing I've recommended when speaking to girls is that they clean up their social media feeds. Rather than following what they find beautiful or pop culture's variations on successful, sexy, or influential, they should first define what those things mean to them.

It would be naive to say a woman shouldn't be concerned with her beauty. Wrong or not, it's where we live and it helps or hinders our confidence, but are we striving for healthy bodies and ideals? We women want to be sexy, beautiful, desirable—but are such expectations realistic? Are our goals attainable, or will they create more negative self-talk in the future? What does a thirteen-year-old girl hate now that she may grow to love about herself after time and maturity?

When I first realized the influence all the fit moms were having on my self-esteem, I scrolled through all my feeds and sat with each account for a moment. I recognized that yogis made me feel inspired because, dear God, all I've ever wanted to be able to do in life is a handstand. Their feeds were primarily about persevering and accepting the person you are each day, the person who is moving a little closer to a goal. They made me smile.

I even showed my daughter one account in particular. "Look at that crazy handstand. She's so strong! I want to be strong like that one day. Wouldn't it be cool to be able to do a handstand on a surfboard in the ocean?"

On the other hand, when I looked at the fit mom accounts, the only words I could think of were skinny, hot, and *I'm going to be single forever*. Unfollow.

I also looked at the women role models who taught me less about body image and more about how I wanted to show up in the world. I had no patience for man haters or women who shamed others or used biting words. I now surround myself with strong, compassionate women who know when and how to take charge and when to be vulnerable.

We should align our social media feeds with the characteristics we choose to build our lives around.

It was recently reported that Oprah Winfrey doesn't allow noise into her home that she hasn't consciously invited. There's no TV or radio in the background because she recognizes that it affects her spirit. How much more so for the things that are attached to our hands for most of the day and those individuals we bring into our lives? The background noise of life affects our spirit.

## Do the Work
## Unfollow, Unfriend, Unload

Our first step is to clean up the messages we receive daily, and that includes our social media feeds, our favorite magazines, blogs, and any content we're feeding on. I use the gut-check method. It's very simple. I go with that little voice inside that I ignore far too often.

When you look at a feed, are you immediately inspired to be the best version of yourself, or do you feel a lack?

Do you wish you were that person and find yourself berating who you are today?

What does your gut tell you about the message you're receiving?

Does it feed a mean-girl itch? Be honest. Look deeper.

If it makes you feel anything remotely negative, click that unfollow button without a second thought. It's not rocket science. There's no need to question why. Believe in your intuition.

Now actively select the women you want to model your life after. Seek out the women who lead by example, who make you feel strong and inspired. Follow. Repeat.

Feed your soul through your feed.

— CHAPTER 22 —

*Your Relationship WITH Self*

*My primary relationship is with myself. All others are mirrors of it.*
—*Shakti Gawain*

**W**omen take on very nurturing, big-sister tones when addressing their younger selves. The very nature of women—feminine grace and a maternal, nurturing spirit—kicks in, and we gently redirect the younger version of ourselves. *You didn't know better. It gets easier. Stop being so hard on yourself. It wasn't your fault. Forgive yourself.*

The first time I saw this phenomenon was in CBS New York News anchor Jessica Moore's letter. I asked her about it when I interviewed her on camera. She said, "If we could only be as gentle with ourselves now, the same way we were when we wrote to our younger selves, how much better we could be."

Negative self-talk is many times the culprit, and it's become more prevalent with the advent of advertising and mirrors. Prior to the Industrial Revolution, the diaries of American girls spoke of their desires to be kind of heart, gracious, and studious. That was before we valued beauty over character. As mirrors became more readily available and were hung in homes and advertisers started to hawk beauty creams and potions, we started a rapid cultural decline in values and self-image. Women are now expected to immediately bounce back from giving birth, never age, and become what men desire most when watching Coors Light ads. We are conditioned by it before we sign up for our first social media account. It's in the lines at the grocery stores and pedaled to our girls from the moment they say the word pink.

So how do we fight it before it gets us? I struggle with the lines sneaking their way onto my face and the softness of my belly, where my daughter grew. I will consciously catch myself looking at models on Instagram and think, I wish I looked like that.

But why?

## Thigh Gap versus Boss

As a society, we receive messages daily. As mentioned above, they are sometimes generational; they are stories about us that come from our families. They determine our belief system, how we worship, whom we respect, gender roles, and right versus wrong. Whether our parents are feminists and forward thinkers, our impressions of ourselves are baked into messages that span centuries. They are far more subliminal and cultural than we consciously recognize. They are a hum that is timeless and unseen.

Some messages come from ad men who figured out how to make you want, consume, and be moved. They have studied your psychology to make money for their employers. This to me is far more dangerous especially for women and girls. Women are utilized as objects and are many times advertised as only limbs or provocatively posed to make the viewer believe that if you consume certain products, you will have the opportunity to consume such a woman.

If you are a woman, of course you want to be like the one in the ad because that is desirable and you should also want to be consumed. To be desirable, we are told to eat clean, never let them see you sweat, be goddesses, and ladies in the streets but freaks in the sheets. Let's throw in the role of PTA mom for good measure. Any good mom knows that being a sexpot and the mother of a toddler requires a lot of dry shampoo and crying.

From the time a girl enters this world, her self-esteem has been prepackaged for her in ways she will never consciously understand; they will be sold to her via advertising, her family's biases and cultural viewpoints, and those that come by way of social influence. She won't have a chance to form her own opinions about who she is in the world. With the ever-expanding reach of social media and viral content, we can't curb this, but we can use our awareness to create a healthy relationship with ourselves through appropriate filters and boundaries.

I recently researched the #bossgirl hashtag while prepping for a speech I was giving to a group of teen girls on social influence. My motivation was to find examples of role models you select and role models that surreptitiously select you. I'd recognized that even my social media feeds required cleaning so I wouldn't fill my mind with images of what was unreasonable for a working mother who was actively quashing negative self-talk.

If looking at a feed made me feel fat or unkempt, or if I heard even an inkling of *Why can't I look like that?* I immediately unfollowed the account. I made a personal vow to follow only those accounts that left me feeling inspired. And I decided to help the room of teen girls do the same. Instead of finding a plethora of social media sites with women who have achieved, who want to inspire others, I found page after page of women with very nice butts. In many of the images, they were posed with men who clearly wanted to consume them. As with most things, I fast-forwarded to the moment my daughter became aware of the image of a strong, confident woman in a society that has become conditioned to think that being desirable is a goal, that thigh gaps were to be maintained, and that you can still be a #boss, no pressure. I thought of the room of twelve- to seventeen-year-old girls who wanted to be something other than lush rear ends. Then I got mad and emailed my creative director, "I dare you to find something under #bossgirl we can show these girls that is not pornographic."

Reality stars, celebrities, and starlets have something to sell—a book, an image, a performance, a TV show—something. I worry that we are not fully aware of the intent of the people we model. To say they are effective is an understatement. I have used MAC's Whirl lip liner for something like ten years. Kylie Jenner posted a photo of her lips and her liner and MAC instantly sold out. For months. I had to go in search of a new color, creature of comfort that I am, and realize that she didn't have just a following. She had a pulpit.

Once you begin to dig, you find that women have been hit from all angles and that you need to be really aware to buffer whom you aspire to be from whom you are told to be. The line is thin. The awareness is so slight and quiet. Whether we are younger or older mothers, our daughters are far more at risk than we were at their age, and we have to help them navigate this awareness.

According to Sally Curtin, a statistician with the National Center for Health Statistics, suicide rates are climbing for every age group under seventy-five since 1999, and the most concerning is girls between the ages of ten and fourteen. Though they make up a very small portion of total suicides, the rate at which they are extinguishing their young lives has tripled over the past fifteen years. While they can't attribute it to any one factor, it is suggested that the earlier onset of puberty and depression may be a cause.

Aside from the pressures that arise when boys and periods show themselves and tendencies are no longer childlike yet nowhere quite near womanly, these girls receive a constant stream of information about whom the world thinks they should be. Other data suggests that at the same moment they are being told they should have a thigh gap and rock the perfect pout, attainment and corner offices await them.

We're at a crossroads. Women and girls are receiving old-world messages about love, parenting, marriage, career attainment, having it all, balance, and what a "normal" life looks like. They are also receiving new-world advertisements that ask them to consume or be consumed and Kardashian messages that sell God knows what. And now, new voices are speaking out. We need our women and girls to rise above the chatter and move our world forward.

It starts with each of us doing the internal work and then finding the words to guide our daughters and friends.

## Do the Work
## Mirror, Mirror

To make sure Olivia develops a strong foundation of self when the mean girls come knocking, I created an inventory of things she knows about herself. She knows she is smart, funny, kind, and pretty. We talk about looks being a blessing, a gift, but the real gems are the parts of her soul and mind that make her formidable. When she has trouble with a bully taunting her about things untrue, I ask her, "What things do you know about yourself?" and we get through it pretty easily.

What do we have as women when the world comes knocking? What things do we know about ourselves?

You'll need a full-length mirror, Post-it notes, and self-love for this exercise.

- What are your positive attributes?

- Are you kind?

- Gracious?

- Intelligent?

- Funny?

- Loving?

- Charitable?

- Genuine?

- Strong?

- Athletic?

- Curvy? Voluptuous?

- Abundant?

- Powerful?

Now, write "I am …" and enter your attributes on Post-it notes. Each should have a separate "I am …" sentence. Stick them to your mirror.

Next, get naked. Yep. I hate this part too, but Oprah Winfrey does it, which means we have to do it. At least until we don't see what we hate about ourselves first. We are conditioning ourselves to see those I am sentences first. We are all those things. I am finally at the place where I can look in a mirror fully clothed and say "I am powerful, I am beautiful, I am strong, I am smart" straight off the bat. I even smile at myself when I first catch my reflection. It still takes a few seconds when I'm naked, but I get there. I invite you to join me.

Oprah has been very open about her body issues. On the stage of one of her Super Soul Sessions, she explained how cathartic it was for her to stand naked in front of the mirror and instead of tearing her body apart, thanking it. Thank your strong legs for carrying you through life. Thank your breasts and belly for feeding and growing the people whom that body created. Thank your skin, thank your arms, thank your earth suit as model and author Emily Nolan calls it, for holding your soul. It's your vehicle, not your destination.

As I was sharing this exercise with my creative director recently, he laughed and told me he heard of a pop-up swim shop somewhere on the West Coast that put Post-its on the mirrors in the dressing rooms with affirmations during swimsuit season. I shook my head. "We've been trying to get the mirror to talk back to us for decades."

It's time. Damn the ad man.

## CHAPTER 23

I t's a rare gem of a woman who has figured out how to sit comfortably in her femininity while masterfully commanding respect from her male peers. This woman chooses her whole self as she enters the workforce. While my experience has always been in corporate America, many of my writers have come from the worlds of media, entertainment, and advertising. From interviews and letters, I have found that the way a woman shows up at work or in relationships has more to do with her perceptions of self based on her childhood and early messages surrounding sexuality and relationships. The environment she chooses to work in may also have something to do with her vacillation between masculinization versus sexualization.

Masculinizing yourself is to make your character, quality, or appearance masculine. We see this many times when a woman dresses more like a man in the work environment, appears more aggressive, or finds ways to subconsciously or consciously divorce her gender. Women do this for a number of reasons including acceptance, power, and avoidance.

To sexualize yourself is to make your character, quality, or appearance sexual for the same reasons. This can move from dress, demeanor, and subtleties to flirtation and more. Some may refer to it as using their feminine "wiles" to accomplish their tasks or desires, but I argue that our divine feminine strengths, the woman in the middle of this spectrum, is in our abilities to influence, nurture, and create balance.

I think it fitting that as I edit this book, Time magazine named the "Silence Breakers" who came forward as part of the #metoo movement its Persons of the Year. The year 2017 has offered us a deep study into the workplace and the lingering toxic masculinity that is ever present. The roots of toxic masculinity are the culprit that provokes our need to show up as anything other than ourselves. We often masculinize ourselves to be heard and to remain in favor but also to avoid sexual overtures or innuendo. If we're one of the guys, we're less likely to be harassed.

Women who overtly sexualize themselves usually do so in order to be seen. They believe they wield influence because they can attract and keep the attention of the men at the table.

This is not to say that any of the women who have come forward have taken part in either. They may enter the workforce as their whole selves, but somewhere along the way, they've been targeted or misused, and their stories reflect a change in the way they interact with men in the workplace. These show themselves as hypervigilance when they are close to men, distrust, and deafening silence that is only now beginning to find an audience.

I worry for the next generation of women entering the workforce. I have been overjoyed with the collective voice of women coming forward. My daughter will go to work in a world much different from the one I went to work in, and I take comfort in that.

I can't blame Pamela Anderson for her recent comments that any woman asked to visit a man's hotel room "knows what she's getting into." Sadly, that statement is made through the lens of someone who had been the victim of sexual violence early in life. She had the hypervigilance and distrust down, but many young women enter the workforce innocent of such things. They want to believe they are talented and look for mentors, not lovers.

I chose the tack of masculinization when I began my ascent through the ranks of corporate America. I was eighteen, and I had no idea I'd be with the same company for over twenty years. Finance is extremely male dominated; as I began to collect titles, I realized I had to lose my softness. I learned how to talk the boys' talk, and I never used my sexuality to attract attention. I was behind the scenes when my male peers talked about the women who did. I vowed never to join their ranks. I wanted to be seen as decisive, respectable, and strong. Those were not the words used to describe women who relied on their looks or those damn feminine wiles when they left the room.

When we women do leave the room, we are finally able to be ourselves. I wasn't fully aware of how deeply we pretend when we are around our male counterparts until I attended Barron's Top Women Advisors in West Palm Beach when Olivia was a baby. With very few men in the room, the women came together in an almost beautiful crescendo of support and conversation. We talked about the guilt we felt raising our children and then pretending to forget them and our gender when we were in boardrooms. We talked about health and fertility issues that we hid from our colleagues because we didn't want them to see us as women. How maternity leave had a stigma attached. It was uncomfortable admitting that we had to leave in order to be mothers, the antithesis of our understanding of success.

Jamie Little, Fox Sports reporter, and a Love Letters contributor, decided early on that she wanted respect from men and felt she had to masculinize herself to garner it. In her interview, she recognized that it may have had to do with the fact her father had been absent in her life, and she wanted to be seen by men as capable and strong. She wore turtlenecks, pulled her hair back in a ponytail, and divorced her femininity so they would see her not as a woman trying to be a man but as a capable reporter.

She also recognized that becoming a married woman helped her in the eyes of male counterparts as she was taken more seriously as opposed to when she was "a single girl." Only after a decade in the field of motorsports reporting, accolades from colleagues, and taking on a new role as a mother did she finally feel comfortable dressing like a woman and showing her femininity. She had to finally garner the respect of those leading the field before she could be seen as her whole self.

On the other side of the spectrum, those whose parents treated conversations around their bodies and sexuality as something women offer men, found themselves sexualizing themselves or entering unhealthy and primarily one-sided relationships.

What I learned from all these letters and multiple workshops is that no two women had the same motivation or approach in their interactions with men. We are all so complex and come with layers of stories and experiences that generalizing or offering psychological buckets would be downplaying the human experience.

Above all else, I noticed that whether a woman leans right or left—masculinization vs. sexualization—far fewer women are completely comfortable somewhere in the middle, in their divine femininity.

Women have a steady stream of thoughts that occur in each situation as they try to offer the face that will be best received, the one that won't get them called a bitch, a slut, a cold fish, frigid, or any of the other descriptors we imagine when we have something important to say.

When we do raise our voices, we are often unclear how we are being received and wonder if there is a point to our collective song. I argue that there is room for every note and melody. Whether that includes fists raised in marches to make a statement or utilizing our empathic abilities to guide a powerful man to our plight, it's most important that we keep talking. We must commune. We must continue to use our self-awareness and intuition to determine what audience needs to hear which tone. But be silent? Never.

I have seen the catalyzing force of company-sponsored women's groups, advocacy projects, and activism. They are all powerful in their own right, and when used masterfully, they accomplish the goal of building communities of women, support, infrastructure, advocacy, and policy reform.

Never doubt your power.

**Do the Work**
**The Feminine Spectrum**

Understand how and why your messaging and environment color the way you show up in the workplace. Where are you on the feminine spectrum?

- Do you masculinize yourself?

- Do you sexualize yourself?

- Do you find yourself choosing one gender over another? Speaking negatively of women or making disparaging remarks about men?

- Are you comfortable in your divine feminine power without vacillating between roles to be heard?

- How do you feel men respond to you in the workplace?

- How would you like men to respond to you in the workplace?

Start there.

I would love to offer answers to these questions to help women feel their roles as women in the workplace more deeply, but the workplace hasn't evolved to that space yet. We have a long way to go and centuries of gender misconceptions and messaging to deconstruct.

But the #metoo movement is offering unprecedented progress. So take heart.

# Part II Key Takeaways

- Determine what you are currently putting off or avoiding that the deathbed you will be thoroughly annoyed by. Create a plan.

- Understand how you can do a better job of choosing yourself in your friendships and relationships.

- Learn to trust yourself. Listen to your intuition, and trust the physical manifestations of those signals.

- Enact healthy boundaries and utilize conflict for good. Speak up for yourself.

- Discover the reasoning behind any need for approval, and work to heal it from the inside out.

- Pay attention to how social media and influence affects you. Unfollow, unfriend, unload.

- Consider the ways you show up in your relationships with men and whether a shift is necessary from masculinization or sexualization to the wonder that is you.

— CHAPTER 24 —

The Letters: MAKING Choices

I curated this grouping of letters specifically because of their pointed advice and the overarching message that we can indeed choose the lives we want, the messaging we create, and our new way forward. We have the power.

## The Letter That Started It All

*Jessica Moore*

Dear Jessica,

I know you love lists, so I'll try to make this unsolicited advice less painful than you think it will be. At least read the list; you don't have to follow everything. Just read the list. And before you read the list, listen to, "Ooo Child." These lyrics will serve as the thread that ties all this advice together.

1.  Sunlight is the best disinfectant. Don't make decisions until you've had a good night's sleep and a long walk outside.
2.  Don't touch your eyebrows. Today's Frida Kahlo is tomorrow's Brooke Shields. And while we're on the topic, do not have the mole on your face removed. Pretty soon, you'll realize that being unique is one of the only things any of us really has.
3.  Many overwhelming problems will become quite simple after an hour on your yoga mat.
4.  Treat the mailman/janitor/barista the same way you treat your best friend.
5.  You will endure pain that you're certain will be the end of you, but it won't be. Hang in there one more day than you think is humanly possible.

The ache is always the most exquisite just before it subsides.

6. The five pounds you've gained that are threatening to throw off your whole diet? No one can see them. Everyone does, however, see the frown on your face as you labor over this nonissue. Get over it.

7. Choose the man who wipes away your tears instead of the one who makes you cry. Choose brains over beauty and a sense of humor over almost anything else. (And don't choose any man at all until you're happy with the woman you see when you look in the mirror.)

8. Get a dog as soon as possible. A dog will help you understand your capacity to love and nurture like nothing else. A dog will also remind you that you're not alone in this world even when you feel you are. Trust me on this. Get a dog.

9. Trust your gut and guard it voraciously. Your instincts will always point you in the right direction. When you're afraid, do it anyway.

10. Be kind and supportive of other women. Not many of your peers will understand the value of this, but those who do will be unstoppable.

11. People will tell you it can't be done. They'll say your dreams are grandiose. Don't listen. Replace your discouragement with compassion and the understanding that those words come only from someone who never had the courage to fail.

12. Finally, let life unfold organically. "When you let things come and you let things go, you let things BE."

It's all going to be so much better than you imagine it will be, Boo. You got this.

Love,


Me


*Jessica Moore is an Emmy award–winning anchor for the weekend evening newscasts on CBS 2 and WLNY 10/55. Moore joined the stations in July 2016. Her broadcasting career has taken her all over the country from WDTN in Dayton, Ohio, to WLEX in Lexington, Kentucky, and most recently KSNV in Las Vegas, Nevada, where she spent six years as the station's primary weekday evening anchor.*

*Her work has earned her two Emmy awards and an Associated Press award. In Lexington, Moore made her network debut on CNN during the Northpoint Prison riots, and she reported for the Weather Channel when a massive snowstorm pounded Kentucky.*

*In 2009, a deadly tornado ripped through parts of central Kentucky. Moore was awarded an Emmy for her spot news coverage of the storm's aftermath. She moved to New York from Las Vegas, where she was nominated for nine Pacific Southwest Emmy awards including best news anchor and best live-event anchoring. She anchored countless hours of live breaking news and election coverage and scored an exclusive interview with Mitt Romney during the 2012 presidential election.*

*Active in the community, she is a passionate advocate for animals. Previously, Moore focused her volunteer efforts with the Make a Wish Foundation of southern Nevada.*

*A native of North Carolina, Moore is a graduate of Liberty University, where she obtained a singing scholarship and earned a bachelor of science degree in psychology.*

# Jamie Little

Jamie Little is one of the toughest women I've ever met. I have many times joked that if there is ever an apocalypse—zombie or otherwise—we would survive if Jamie were on our team. In her love letter to her younger self, she speaks candidly of her rise in the male-dominated field of sports announcing and her relationship with her father.

Ladies and gentlemen, the very badass Jamie Little -

I was a strong-minded, only child raised by a single mom. For some reason, I always had gumption. I was always brave and never afraid. Maybe it was growing up in the outdoor paradise that is South Lake Tahoe, California. Maybe it was having a strong mom who never took no for an answer. Maybe it was not having a father around to give me the idea that I needed a man to do things for me.

Whatever it may be, that strong, independent spirit has never let me down. It's led me astray at times and gotten me in trouble a time or two, but it always brought me back to the "right" path. With that, here's a letter to my younger self, a list of explanations you could say. This is for the girl who loved horses, loved boys (at a very young age!), never settled for no, loved her mom to a fault, and missed having a father, her father, more than she could accept until much later in life.

Dear Jamie:

Don't be ashamed that you don't have a dad around. Most of your friends at your young age still have two-parent households, but it's okay to have the love of two parents wrapped in one. You'll use that void left by your father to fuel your passion to succeed in a male-dominated world such as motorsports television. You'll yearn to have acceptance by men for your character, hard work, and accomplishments. You'll get it.

Your love for racing isn't weird! Your friends and classmates won't understand why you will start bringing dirt-bike magazines to class in high school. Your mom will be shocked one day to discover all your precious, innocent horse posters have been replaced by dirt bikes, racers, and autographs. It's okay that you don't have a brother or father around to promote something like dirt bikes. One day, everyone will understand your love and passion for something so rough and "unladylike."

Those tears, lonely nights, on the road, and small paychecks will all be part of the plan. Suck it up, and keep your eye on the prize. The more you endure and the harder you work selflessly, the bigger the reward. It'll all lead to true happiness, but it'll be a long road. Keep digging.

Don't sweat the small stuff, and trim the fat while you're at it. Your stepmother may have "taken" your father away and tried to keep you out, but being angry, sad, and disappointed won't help. Just accept your relationship with your father for what it is—surface conversation between two blood acquaintances. Ironically, the day will come that you are all your father will have. You'll end up burying his wife. That will leave him alone, broke, and depressed with nobody but you to lean on. Take it as God's work to be there. Don't judge. Don't walk away. Be there. You'll be your father's shining light in his darkest days. Funny how life works out sometimes.

You always wanted a baby brother or sister. Though that won't happen, one day, you'll have the chance to hold, love, and care for a baby of your own. It'll be hard to fathom while you're keeping your nose to the grindstone and hardly coming up for air, but it'll happen. Just be sure to open your heart, enjoy dating, and don't take yourself so seriously.

In the end, it's not all about your career or becoming wealthy though those things are nice; it's all about the circle of family you create around you. So don't wait too long, but don't settle either. Oh, and don't keep people in your life just because. Cut those who are toxic, dramatic, or energy zappers. Life is too short. Keep your circle tight.

Don't be labeled. In life, people will want to characterize you into a category. "She's a pretty girl. She's a tomboy. She's a hardass. She's a classy lady. She's a partier. She's a country-club type of woman." Don't be afraid to be all things. You will be a woman who can wear a dress and heels and interview anyone on TV. You will be a country girl who loves country music, cold beer, and swearing. You'll like riding dirt bikes, and you'll enjoy golf. You'll hang with millionaires while sipping expensive wine. You'll also wear your sweats and feed the homeless on D Street or walk homeless dogs in the impoverished part of town. Be all things. Life is so much more exciting that way.

Respect your mom. She'll drive you crazy, and you'll drive her crazy. You'll be angry at her and hold grudges for things she did as a parent. But let it go. The only important thing is that you have each other. She'll be your number-one fan your whole life. She'll be your cheerleader when you call her with self-doubt and disappointment. She's done it all. She's your best resource. Stay close to her always. Help her in times of need. She'll need you in a big way.

Her husband, who you call Pops, will see the bitter side of life. He'll one day look at death in the face, but his attitude and the love of you mother will steer him away. It'll end up being the biggest challenge in all your lives. Stick together. It's the only way.

Love,


Jamie

*Veteran motorsports reporter Jamie Little joined FOX NASCAR in 2015 for its fifteenth season and brought thirteen years of broadcasting experience and a lifetime of racing knowledge to her pit reporting duties in the NASCAR Sprint Cup series and NASCAR Xfinity series.*

Her assignments also include select additional races and special events throughout the year.

Prior to joining FOX, Little spent thirteen years at ESPN/ABC as a reporter for NASCAR (2007–2014), IndyCar Series (2004–2014), Winter X Games, and Summer X Games telecasts.

Her television career began in 2002 as a reporter for ESPN immediately following graduation from college. She also has worked for SPEED, NBC, and TNN. Her move to FOX after multiple years with ABC and ESPN represents a homecoming of sorts for Little. She covered a variety of motorsports events for FOX Sports' SPEED in 2002 and 2003 including the network's live coverage of the Daytona Supercross, which marked her live national broadcasting debut.

She was the first female pit reporter for the TV broadcast of the prestigious Indianapolis 500 in 2004 and the first female to cover televised supercross and motorcross events; she was also one of the first female reporters in X Games history.

Little has covered eleven Indianapolis 500s and eight Brickyard 400s, and she has hosted a variety of nonracing sporting events ranging from paintball championships to the Great Outdoor Games in addition to live announcing roles in motorcross and supercross.

Little credits her lifelong passion for the sport and affinity for dirt bikes as being the springboard for her entry into television. While still in college, she reported on various motorsports for ESPN2 and served as a live announcer in supercross events.

The Las Vegas resident is well rounded outside the four corners of a race track as well. In 2013, she released her first book, Essential Car Care for Women, and she has worked the red carpet for the ESPYs in addition to hosting numerous NASCAR events away from the track.

*The popular racing video game "MX World Tour Featuring Jamie Little" bears her name and likeness. She also held a cameo role in the 2005 feature film Fantastic Four and Supercross the Movie starring Channing Tatum.*

*Little spends her free time volunteering at the Animal Foundation, Nevada's largest animal rescue shelter. Her first solo charity project was a 2016 calendar titled "Las Vegas to the Rescue" featuring Las Vegas celebrities such as Wayne Newton, Carrot Top, and NASCAR driver Brendan Gaughan; she posed with homeless pets from the shelter to promote adoption.*

*A graduate of San Diego State University with a degree in journalism, Little grew up in South Lake Tahoe, California. She resides in Las Vegas with her husband and son. You can follow Jamie on Twitter at @ JamieLittleTV.*

# Amy Jo Martin

Amy Jo Martin is a self-proclaimed renegade. Anyone who meets her in person would agree wholeheartedly. Her ideas have power and form and have become legendary whether it is her entrepreneurial pursuits, her mentorship of Girls for Progress, her speaking engagements, or most recently, the evolution of her "Why Not Now?" podcast from curiosity to raging success.

Dear Young Amy Jo:

I write this letter to you on a plane as I fly back to US soil after spending time in Asia. As I boarded the plane in Hong Kong, another mass shooting in the US was topping global news. The more we're exposed to in this world, the more we realize how little we know or understand. That said, please take what's useful from this advice and leave behind what isn't. You will create your own journey that will make you unique.

Btw, we're quite stubborn, and it's possible you won't listen to the advice below. Regardless, you will still live a fulfilling life (at least until you're thirty-six). We think in bullet points and absorb content best in the form of bullet points, so here goes.

- You'll experience some amazing things. Humble yourself or the universe will do that for you. The world is much bigger than we are, and it doesn't revolve around us. The people we respect the most including our mentors are the humblest people we'll ever meet.

- We can't bank sleep—we can't deposit hours into a fictitious sleep account and withdraw rest when needed. That strategy simply won't net out well regardless of what grades we earn in math. After averaging four to five hours a night for several years, our thirty-six-year-old version has finally learned to respect sleep. She guards it fiercely. I encourage you to protect your sleep at a younger age. (P.S.: math is one of our sweet spots. It's our jam. We like black-and-white answers and scenarios. This poses challenges for us. Read on.)

- Learn to push your buttons. Inspire yourself. Everyone else is busy. It's wonderful and convenient when others inspire us, but there will be droughts between the supply and the demand. Subsidizing with a self-sufficient supply of inspiration serves as our safety net. This is how we make inspiration sustainable and scalable. Personally, our strongest source of inspiration is nature—being outdoors.

- In third grade, you will be put in a special reading and writing class because you're not quite performing up to par with your classmates. Accept, listen, and learn. We will apply these skills years down the road when we write our first New

York Times bestselling book. We must always appreciate the opportunities we are given to slow down, listen, and learn. Timing is everything. Trust the process.

- Where purpose, passion, and skill collide, bliss resides. This sounds like fluffy BS, but it's your reason for not worrying about knowing what path or profession you'll want to choose when you enter college. Just be open. Try everything, and listen to how you feel. Purpose. Passion. Skill. Collide them. (A heads-up here: they change, so don't get too comfy.)

- Don't let other people take up space in your head for free; that's valuable real estate. What other people think of you is none of your business. Be you and let go. Repeat. This is a tough one for us. It requires constant practice. We struggle and trip over this one at times.

- Learn when to make things happen instead of letting things happen. When you feel strongly about something, move confidently in that direction. If you don't like that path after you've given it a red-hot go, simply choose again. If you're torn between letting something happen or making it happen, sit down at the fork in the road and pause. Hint: we have a tendency to make things happen and even force them at times. Ease up, sister.

- Getting comfortable with being uncomfortable is extremely powerful, but it takes daily practice. Take risks. When in doubt, ask yourself, What's the worst thing that could happen if I try _____? And then what? And then what? Also ask, Is _____ safe enough to try?

- Read. Read. Read. Make it a part of your day, your world. Surround yourself with people who also love to read. Give books as gifts. The benefits are unmatched.

- Travel. Even if it's an hour from where you live. Exploring will open your mind. If you have an opportunity to travel due to your career, take the ticket and explore while working and especially while you're young and have fewer geographic anchors. Don't spend thirty-six hours in Australia for the first time because it's supposed to be a "quick" work trip. Add a few more days and explore. Chances are that nobody will question the request. Hint: you just have to ask.

- Words matter. With all relationships, exchange we with me as much as possible.

- Try not to worry so much about your career, your weight, your finances, your future, and so on. It will all work out. We're warriors, not worriers.

- Your career will take off, but please, please don't get caught up in it. Make family a priority. I didn't attend my grandmother's funeral because I had a business trip that was supposedly critical to my career. We are one of nineteen grandchildren, and only two of us didn't make it to the funeral. To this day, I can't remember what that very important, career-altering opportunity was. Show up for family. It matters.

- Be kind and smile. It's good for the soul, it's a mood-changer, it's contagious, and it attracts. Kindness and smiles are the ultimate positive boomerangs.


I love you, and I hope you learn to love yourself at an earlier stage than I did.

Ajo

*Amy Jo is the author of the New York Times bestseller Renegades Write the Rules and host of the Why Not Now? podcast. She has a social media following of more than 1.1 million and was named the third most powerful woman on Twitter by Forbes. She believes that the future of technology is the future of humanity. Amy Jo conducts clinical research studies and travels the world to speak about this topic and many others.*

*She founded Digital Royalty in 2009 to help corporations, celebrities, and sports entities humanize their brands online through social communication channels. Amy Jo has worked closely with world-renowned brands such as Hilton Worldwide, Dwayne "The Rock" Johnson, and Shaquille O'Neal to successfully humanize their presence. Her motto is: Humans connect with humans, not logos.*

*In 2012, Tony Hsieh, CEO of Zappos.com, and Baron Davis, NBA player, invested in Amy Jo and her company. After a successful seven-year run as the founder and CEO of Digital Royalty and growing the business globally into ten countries, Amy Jo recently exited the company.*

*As a young female building her career in male-centric industries, Amy Jo developed a passion for helping women thrive in business leadership roles. She is also a contributor to news outlets including the Harvard Business Review and Sports Business Journal. She has been featured in top-tier media outlets including Vanity Fair, Time, Forbes, the New York Times, Fast Company, ESPN SportsCenter, USA Today, MSNBC, and Newsweek.*

# Sadaf Baghbani

When Sadaf Baghbani isn't traveling the globe due to her wanderlust or the foundations she is setting up for international families; she is giving back to her community and starting her own businesses. A heart of pure gold and the innate desire to leave her imprint on this world make her a force of nature.

Dear Sadaf,

Decades from now, you'll be sitting under the scorching Doha sun with sweat dripping down your neck and wondering if you had made the right decision to pack your stuff only to move across this expansive world to be in a country that's in an economic and political blockade.

This will not be your first move, nor will it be your last. You will pack your bags many times and head to Africa, the Middle East, and lands you never imagine in your youth. You will go to war-torn countries, countries with a slew of economic and political problems, but you'll love every second of it. Every time an opportunity comes knocking, a part of you will question if it's the right move, if it's the safe move. But you'll go, you'll keep your head high, and you'll have the time of your life with stories to pass on for generations.

People will come and go in your life. The key for you will be to remember that each person, good or bad, is there to teach you about humanity, strength, cruelty, and reality. Take what you learn and harness it into the love you feel for this world and the people you want to help. You know that warmth you feel when you help women and girls? Channel that into building the skills that will make you a game changer, a visionary, but most important, a humanitarian.

Remember that this doesn't have to come in the form of a traditional path or in a set time. One day, a girl from the Middle East will tell you her dreams and fears. She will tell you about the ideas she thinks will never happen. Your job will be to help her grow that little flame into a blazing fire of hope and determination. You will help her harness all her dreams and show her they can all come true.

There will be days when you'll be waiting for the next door to open. You'll feel completely lost and afraid that maybe this recent adventure is where your luck will run out. But take your tattered journals and keep them close to your heart. When you need to, write, sketch, or paint what you experience. These will fill many plastic bins that you'll look through hundreds of times to remind you of why you go on these grand adventures to the unknown.

You'll sit on a bus one day riding across the green, endless Drakensburg Mountains while reading Cry, the Beloved Country and will weep for everyone's history and past. When you feel embarrassed that you've felt so deeply about a cause that is not yours, remember that your empathy is unique; it will have brought you there. You will use your empathy to affect the people you meet.

In an unsafe world, remember that there are people who are good and there are people who are afraid. When you meet these people, remember that though you might not be able to change their experiences, you can listen and maybe in the slightest way help them.

One day, you will meet an elderly man who is a forced migrant from Zimbabwe with no place to turn and who sadly but without intention shares his story. Don't think twice when you give him your last $200 to help him get across the country in hopes of a job. This encounter will leave the deepest imprint on your soul. When you do something as simple as an ATM transaction to provide a little comfort to someone though you're down to your last couple bucks and you've called your sister to wire you some money to get you home while you sit and wonder if you've made the right move, just know that you did. One day, he will write you that he's found a job, made a new home, and has found his soul mate.

Finally, there will be nights when you weep and feel utterly alone in a world full of people. You'll worry that you haven't followed a traditional path that anchors you to a place. But that nagging feeling you constantly feel when you're home that there are people you need to meet, experiences you need to have, and places you need to see—that feeling will never go away. Accept with an open mind and heart that this might just be your destiny right now and that it's all right. You'll be fine.

With love and loyalty,


Your older self


*Sadaf Baghbani immigrated to the United States soon after the end of the Iran-Iraq war. She holds a bachelor's of science degree in biology and political science as well as a master's degree in public policy and global management.*

*She has spent time in South Africa as part of the US Department of Education's Fulbright program for McNair scholars to conduct independent research on skills development among HIV-positive men as well as development and grant production for charities throughout southern Africa. She then worked with the Jordan Institute of Diplomacy in the Regional Centre for Conflict Prevention, where she conducted firsthand research on conflict in the Levant region.*

Sadaf's passion for philanthropy and business recently took her to Qatar, where she helped create a family foundation and other businesses for the royal family.

She lives in Las Vegas, where she co-launched with her sister the Bridged Agency, a global online business advisory firm that focuses on women's empowerment.

PART THREE

*The Future //:*

MANIFEST

*The best way to predict the future is to create it.*
—*Abraham Lincoln*

## CHAPTER 25

Manifesting

**W**hat if I told you that you are powerful beyond measure? That everything you could possibly want lies within your grasp?

The ability to manifest is available to everyone. It offers you the power to intentionally create the life you desire.

I know. It's hard to imagine when you're clocking in, eating Ramen, and wondering how you'll make ends meet this month. If I were to sit in front of you today and tell you that the world was at your fingertips, you'd roll your eyes and hope I choked on my silver spoon. But here's the funny part. I got where I am out of sheer will. I wished myself into this spot.

My start looked a lot different from my daughter's. I recently took Olivia home to Florida to see her grandfather, and on the way to Busch Gardens, I asked her, "Do you want to see where I grew up?"

"Yes," she said.

"When we get there, I'll slow down, but I can't stop. It's not a very safe neighborhood, so you'll have to pay attention when I point out the house to you."

"Mom, why would you take me somewhere that wasn't safe?"

Our neighbors were drug dealers, traffickers, prostitutes, and murderers. I never knew that I could have anything more than what was there, and oh my God, how I couldn't wait to leave. I didn't say that I wanted to become the me I am today; I couldn't have even imagined this woman. No. I visualized myself in comfort and security and always said I wanted just enough to put my children in sports or ballet if they wanted. I manifested myself to freedom, to happiness, to words that didn't have price tags. Here is a secret when you learn how to effectively manifest: the money will follow. You must respect the money. You must respect the abundance and never take it for granted. Be grateful every day for the life you create. It is available to you. You can have anything you want with work and intention.

Start by writing it down. Say it out loud, "I am what I say I am."

When I was a teenager, I would make "What do I want?" lists. It was almost as if my future self was thoroughly annoyed with the me who was whining over an issue and I could hear her say, "Omg, get over yourself! What do you want?"

I wanted all kinds of things. I wanted to travel. I wanted to make $100,000. I wanted to be published. I wanted to ride in a hot-air balloon. The only thing that hasn't happened is the hot-air balloon. I see them every Friday morning in the canyon beyond my house, so to make that last one happen would require a simple phone call.

In my twenties, life was more complicated. I wanted to love someone more than he loved me. I wanted to learn how to trust. I got exactly what I wanted. For better or worse. I loved someone more than he loved me, and I misplaced my trust. As I read my words years later, heartbroken over the end of that relationship, I realized I needed to be a little more specific in my orders. The universe had made good on everything I'd asked for in the course of my writings.

Most recently, this has shown up in other ways. I am a trained public speaker and expert storyteller. Some people are good at math. I'm good at telling stories to large crowds. I was frustrated that I wasn't getting the speaking gigs I'd preferred. I was confident in my gift, so about a year ago, I changed my title on all my social media. Instead of referring to myself as a "writer, lover, and shoe fiend" as I had for years, I changed it to "speaker, author, advocate."

In no time, I was receiving requests to speak at conferences, to women's groups, high school students, and fitness retreats. I simply said it, and it became. I had never thought of myself as a speaker because it wasn't in my job description as part of my professional career. It's a skill I've developed through training, coaching, and practice.

I had lunch with a gentlemen recently who was frustrated that he wasn't being used for his deep knowledge of a specific topic. I challenged him. "You are what you say you are. Just randomly change the way you present yourself to the world. You are a thought leader and expert in—insert your particular skill set here—and see what happens."

I received an email from him shortly thereafter. "I took what you said to heart, and you are right. I needed to own it before others could see me as such."

In my interviews with successful women, I learned very quickly that they knew what they wanted and weren't afraid to speak it into existence even when the first whisperings back to them weren't pleasant. Jessica Moore was advised that she wasn't cut out for the news business six months before she landed an anchor position. She thanked her detractors for strengthening her resolve and even some of her skills before she continued on her path of manifesting what she wanted the most.

Jamie Little had only her hand in a shot on NASCAR weekend as she held the microphone for the drivers and wondered, How do I get on TV? She called the man in charge and shared her desire. Several months later after she'd done an amazing job on a trial basis for very little pay, she threw her hand up for another opportunity and said, "I'd like to do that." That turned into X Games.

The last two promotions I received were because I made those around me aware of my interests and professional goals. Speak your desires to those who can help you, imagine the outcome, and remain indifferent to how it manifests itself. I promise that it will always show up in a much bigger way than you could dream on your own.

**Do the Work**
**The Wish List**

Start your "What Do I Want?" list, which I am now retitling "The Wish List" as a nod to Dr. Wayne Dyer's book Wishes Fulfilled: Mastering the Art of Manifesting. Oddly, I read it on the plane to Maui yesterday, where I am currently writing this chapter while staring at the ocean. I had no idea that Dr. Dyer's sacred writing space was in Maui until I read it in his book, so I feel that this chapter has a bit of magic and blessings attached to it. Perfect wishing conditions.

Manifesting is in your power. You are feeding your subconscious mind with data, and over time, those instructions will become real. Everything I wished for was relatively loose in direction. I wished for success, comfort, security, and a family, and I got all those things. So instead of wishing for the marketing position at Acme Advertising with a parking spot, three weeks' vacation, and a corner office, wish for a successful career in marketing. Or better yet, a successful career that feeds your soul. The rest will follow.

Write down your wishes. Keep them close. Look at them before bed.

Welcome to your power.

## CHAPTER 26

This is the good stuff the Kraken lady referred to, and I wholeheartedly agree. This is where we harness the love letters to visualize success, set goals, and create some good, old-fashioned self-love.

Throughout this book, I've talked about manifesting and how to use your writing practice to move you forward in life. Well, just as we have created relationships with our younger selves, we also have future selves or what some would think of as their higher selves. Our higher selves are very wise, and they adore us. They don't look at us with the marks of judgment, only compassion and excitement.

Remember the compassion you had for your younger self? Well, you are the younger self now. This interaction is pure grace. Your higher self knows what you are capable of and where you are going; she just has to show you the way. You already know her, but you may have just lost sight of her. Maybe your dream of becoming an actress was dashed with an unexpected pregnancy, or you stopped writing that novel because you had to become a caregiver. Life, the messy parts, needed to be lived, and you stopped talking to her because you had lost focus. Today, she will talk back.

**Do the Work**
**Visualizing Your Future (or Higher) Self**

Close your eyes and imagine your future or higher self.

- What does she look like?

- Where is she?

- What is she doing?

- What emotions or characteristics come to mind when you see her?

- What is she like?

- What does she want you to know?

- How do you feel tapping into her?

She knows you. She knows your excuses. She knows your story. She also knows what you are capable of, and she sees through your shit. She can see clearly into your soul. She knows your pain and your stories, and she loves you unconditionally.

- What does she tell you that you need to do to bridge the gap between her and where you are today?

- Do you need to take a class?

- Work on yourself?

- End a relationship?

*Jeanette Schneider*

- Forgive someone or something?

- Learn to love yourself?

- Find your voice?

- Move?

- End a pattern?

- What does your future self, who loves you so much, want you to know?

- How does she spend her time?

- What do her relationships look like?

- What is her relationship to money? To career?

Write it. Make it a statement. Turn it into I ams, build it into wishes for your wish list, co-create with her, and become the you she sees. She looks at you with the same love and tenderness you had when you talked to your younger self, and all she wants is to see you grow and become your very best self.

Next, write a love letter from the perspective of your future (higher) self: dare yourself not to cry or feel so powerful that you can bend steel or eat boys for breakfast.

Do the work. The result is so much sweeter than the solitude of divorcing your stories and experiences or masking them for comfort. That's no good. It makes you wrinkle.

You are magic. Say it. Write it down. Believe it: "I am magic."

# Part III Key Takeaways

- Dear maker, manifestor, create a wish list. Refer to it often.

- Establish a writing practice. Write hard. Write clear. When it hurts, write. When you avoid, write. When you are unable to sleep, write.

- Forgive your younger self, and establish a relationship with your future (higher) self. Only magic can come from such vision.

## CHAPTER 27

**D**onna Brazile had just been named the chair of the Democratic National Committee when she gave the keynote address at the 2016 MGM Grand Resorts Women's Leadership Conference. I sat in the audience raptly listening to her speak of her childhood "Letters to God," an overt exercise in manifesting, and her admonishment that we take time in our busy lives to reflect on how far we've come.

I was also wrestling with my own concerns as she spoke. I was to facilitate a Love Letters workshop on the second day of the conference. I worried I was going to force women to do uncomfortable work. It was a very big departure from the corporate tone of the day. I didn't know how it would be received. I scribbled notes to myself trying to recreate my workshop overnight. I also did a fair amount of praying. I asked for signs that I was on the right track and left it to faith and fate.

Later that evening, Ms. Brazile was seated at a table during the conference VIP reception. She was surrounded by well-wishers, and I had no intention of introducing myself. But a colleague insisted on talking to her, and as we made our way over, there was suddenly a break in the line. I walked directly up to her and said, "Ms. Brazile, I so appreciated your keynote today. I was taken with your 'Letters to God' and your advice that women should take time to reflect on their paths."

She smiled. "I just wrote a letter to my younger self. Would you like to read it?"

My body broke out into goose bumps (a gut-check moment for sure) as I stammered, "I'm talking about this tomorrow."

She handed me her iPad, and I stood in the center of a crowded reception reading her letter while she continued chatting with other guests. Every minute or so, she would look over to check on my progress, and when I was done, my eyes were filled with tears. I explained that I was asking women to do the same, and I asked if she'd be willing to let me share her letter as I opened my session. She hit the email button, handed me her iPad to type in my email address, and the next morning, I read her letter to 250 stunned women who were very willing to do the work with me.

It took me over an hour to get out of the room after my session. Women were lined up to share their stories. I emailed her that night with deep gratitude for how she had unknowingly confirmed my purpose. She was my sign.

# Donna Brazile

Dear Donna,

Sixteen is such a wonderful age. It's the age of novels, when young girls go out in the world for the first time and encounter dangers and obstacles. With perseverance and determination, the young girl overcomes the barriers and perils, matures, and emerges a young woman.

You don't live in a world of such romance. Your world is troubled. There have been riots and agitation, but landmark legislation and a change however slight of the national conscience. In your lifetime, civil rights have taken a quantum leap, and you yourself benefited from Head Start. But there are quantum leaps yet to go. You were witness to assassinations, most twisting that of your inspiration, Martin Luther King.

But like the heroines of yore, you persevered. Even in high school, you were a leader, an independent thinker, an I'm-not-going-to-take-that- "stuff" kind of girl.

Yet the country is at a crossroads. It's reeling, coming out of Vietnam and Watergate. The activism of the 60s has mellowed out at least on the surface. And you— you're at that age of decision, emergence, balancing between childhood and adulthood. What will you make of your life? What direction will you choose? The possibilities are endless and daunting.

You're searching for balance, perspective, direction. What's your mission in life? The sports, the classes, the friends, even the family—they occupy your time, but what occupies your mind is an almost obsession with those questions: What will you do with yourself? What will your mission be? You need inspiration.

And inspiration will come. Let me assure you, let me calm you, let me give you confidence and hope. Inspiration will come. And it will come soon in a way that not only inspires you but also in a sense defines your soul.

The inspiration comes in the form of a speech: Barbara Jordan's keynote address to the Democratic National Convention in 1976. It is the most significant speech of the convention—indeed, you will learn later that it is considered one of the top five American speeches of the twentieth century. And she is speaking about the significance that she, an African-American woman, is speaking before a national audience in such a forum. She is speaking about building a national community, about a belief in the "equality of all and the privilege of none," about being inclusive, not exclusive, about a belief that governance comes from the people, and that the authority of the people should be extended, not restricted, about a belief that government represents the authority of all the people, not just one interest group, and that government has an obligation to "actively seek to remove those obstacles which would block individual achievement," about a belief that traditions inform our decisions but that innovation leads to the future, about a belief that "the gap between the promise and reality of America can one day be finally closed."

And she speaks about so much more. And the voice, the voice has a cadence that could be your own.

You will ask yourself, who is this Barbara Jordan? And you will discover that she became the first African-American Texas state senator since 1883, and the first black woman ever. You will discover that she was the first woman from Texas elected to the House of Representatives. You will discover her speech before the House Judiciary Committee was influential in the process of impeaching Richard Nixon. And of course she was the first African-American woman to deliver a keynote address at the Democratic National Convention.

A woman of so many firsts! You will have other inspirations, other role models, other mentors too numerous to mention here, and many too far in your future. But Barbara Jordan will inspire you to be a woman of many firsts. She will inspire you to dedicate your life to those beliefs—to fight for equality, for inclusiveness, for involvement, for engaging and elevating the public discourse.

My dear Donna at sixteen, listening to Barbara Jordan will be a pivotal moment in your life. The seed of your life's mission will begin to sprout, and you will begin to find words to express and actions to effect those beliefs. And those beliefs will carry you through times of difficulty, hardship, and despair and be with you in times of triumph, achievement, and joy.

Donna

*Veteran political strategist Donna Brazile is the former chair of the Democratic National Committee (DNC) and the author of the New York Times bestseller Hacks: The Inside Story of the Break-Ins and Breakdowns That Put Donald Trump in the White House. She is also the author of the 2004 best-selling memoir Cooking with Grease: Stirring the Pots in American Politics. She is a coauthor of the forthcoming book entitled For Colored Girls Who Have Considered Politics.*

*Ms. Brazile has devoted her life to working for progressive change, responsible governance, and the advancement of all people in a society that is fair and equitable.*

*Brazile first became involved in politics at age nine when she worked to elect a city council candidate who had promised to build a playground in her neighborhood; the candidate won, the playground was built, and a lifelong passion for political progress was ignited.*

*Brazile has worked on every major presidential campaign since 1976, and in 2000, she became the first African-American woman to serve as the manager of a major party presidential campaign, running the campaign of former vice president Al Gore.*

*Ms. Brazile loves working with young people and encouraging them to vote, to run for office, and to work within the system to strengthen it. She has lectured at over 200 colleges and universities across the country on such topics as "Inspiring Civility in American Politics," "Race Relations in the Age of Obama," "Why Diversity Matters," and "Women in American Politics."*

*In 2013, Ms. Brazile was appointed by President Obama to serve on the J. William Fulbright Foreign Scholarship Board. She is also the proud recipient of more than ten honorary doctorate degrees from major colleges and universities including her alma mater, Louisiana State University.*

*In October 2017, Ms. Brazile was the recipient of the WEB Dubois Medal, Harvard's highest honor in African-American studies. Brazile has served as an adjunct professor at Georgetown University since 2002, and she spent the fall of 2017 serving as a Joan Shorenstein fellow in Media, Politics and Public Policy at the Harvard Kennedy School.*

*O, The Oprah Magazine chose Ms. Brazile as one of its twenty "remarkable visionaries" for the magazine's first-ever O Power List. In addition, she was named among the 100 Most Powerful Women by Washingtonian magazine and Top 50 Women in America by Essence magazine, and she received the Congressional Black Caucus Foundation's highest award for political achievement. In 2016, Ms. Brazile was awarded Wonk of the Year from the Kennedy Political Union at American University.*

*Ms. Brazile has worked passionately on behalf of her beloved hometown, New Orleans. In the aftermath of the two catastrophic hurricanes that devastated the gulf region, Ms. Brazile was appointed by former Governor Kathleen Blanco to serve on the Louisiana Recovery Board to work for the rebuilding of the state and to advocate for the gulf recovery on the national* stage. Ms. Brazile was also appointed by former New Orleans Mayor Mitch Landrieu to serve on the Tricentennial Commission.

Ms. Brazile was formerly a contributor to ABC News and CNN and a syndicated newspaper columnist for Universal U'Click. She moonlights as an actress and is especially honored to have made three cameo appearances on CBS's *The Good Wife* and two cameo appearances on Netflix's series *House of Cards*. She most recently appeared on BET's *Being Mary Jane*. Ask her and she'll tell you that acting after all is the key to success in politics.

Ms. Brazile is the founder and director of Brazile & Associates LLC, a general consulting, grassroots advocacy, and training firm based in Washington, DC.

## Priya Matthew

Priya Matthew has a way with words that is otherworldly. A gifted journalist, producer, and storyteller, she creates stories with purpose, and she is an avid learner and life student.

Dear Priya,

I am writing this letter on a train en route to Washington, DC, where I now live. A silhouette of Manhattan's skyline dissolves behind me as I sip piping-hot chai and listen to our favorite album, John Coltrane's A Love Supreme. At twenty-eight, I am still a lone wolf—thoughtful, nostalgic, melancholic, and unsurprisingly old fashioned for a woman my age, which is why I know some things.

There is a season for everything. Pete Seeger made this biblical sentiment come alive for us through his song "Turn, Turn, Turn." The ecclesiastical lesson is simple: there is a time, place, and purpose for all things. Life is a cyclical process. Love, loss, sickness, success, failure—everyone encounters them all. Simply follow your intuition and move forward in faith. Your fear is futile in the battle for control.

Worry about what only the right people think of you. Pay no heed to the actions or words of people who are unkind to you; they will be inconsequential in your life. Instead, focus your energy on folks who build you up. For every naysayer who seeks to make you feel inferior, you will find a friend who affirms your spirit. Invest your emotions in those who are worthy of your love and admiration. Strive to make them proud. You can always go ahead and get even, but do so only with those who have been good to you.

Gratitude is great for your health.

Only our closest confidants will understand the depth of our lifelong struggle with depression. The nature of this pestilence is cruel and often threatens to snuff out the light that burns in us. But I implore you to take heart because we are blessed beyond measure. Meditate on that daily, and then be a rainbow in someone else's cloud as Maya Angelou said. This disease will hinder you at times, but it doesn't have to be a millstone around your neck. Encourage yourself.

Your difference makes you successful.

Comparison can be a thief of joy, but it can also be a powerful impetus for action. We were made to solve the problems that make us angry; we were born to be creative, solicitous, and intense. Dedicate yourself to self-discovery while you're young because good character needs to be developed. Learn to accept your ethnicity, skin color, orientation, and ideology as assets, not impediments. Everything we know and are will be useful in our pursuit of self-actualization.

Live intentionally.

Wake up every morning with a clear sense of intention. In all areas of life, intent determines the outcome of any situation. You should always be willing to take a step back and evaluate why you are doing something. When all else fails, remember the words of the great American playwright John Patrick Shanley, who once advised listening past your first desire to your second. Your second desire speaks less loudly, but she whispers with far more conviction.

Finally, as my train passes through Philadelphia, I bring this letter to a close. I am proud of you, Priya. You're a good kid—kind, generous, loyal, clever. You have an old head on those young shoulders. As you grow older, remember to keep your parents in a place of honor. Support your sister in all her endeavors. Carry on the legacy left to you by your grandparents. I love you.

Yours truly,

pm

*Priya Mathew works at the Washington Post, where she produces interviews and events featuring some of the country's most influential leaders in government, business, medicine, technology, and entertainment. Prior to joining the Post in 2016, she worked in Nevada for veteran political journalist Jon Ralston as the statewide producer for his television program.*

*Her most notable interview subjects include Secretary of State Hillary Clinton, Senator Ted Cruz, Senator Bernie Sanders, Willie Nelson, Deepak Chopra, and Hasan Minhaj.*

# Emily Nolan

I met Emily Nolan through Girls For Progress and watched as she captivated a room full of teenage girls as she spoke about body image. As a successful model dealing with severe body dysmorphia, she spoke of self-love and acceptance. She has become a global voice in self-acceptance.

Dear Emily,

You are eighteen years younger than I am, and you're already so incredibly smart, strong, and beautiful inside and out. You are the greatest gift God has given the world, and you are perfect just the way you are. You were born to be a brave leader. And most important, you're a fierce lover. You lead with love so divinely well; it's a special gift you'll always have unlimited access to. Use love as much as possible.

Dear warrior, use your bravery to listen to who you are throughout the years. There will be challenging moments that will sadly make your heart break, and you'll need to be there to love yourself fiercely. You'll need your friends and family too to lean on for help because you can't do everything always. Sometimes, you'll need help. Everyone does.

Those moments of listening to yourself feel like listening to your gut and choosing not to believe a bully's or someone else's unremarkable opinion of whom they think you should be or what you should look like. Later in life, you'll know those brave moments to be God's grace, which is also your divine grace.

You're a child of God, Emily. Your parents' divorce, the bullying at school, and other moments to come that might make you feel icky and sad inside do not decide your worthiness. God does. You do. And because you get to decide what a miracle you are, continue to be brave enough to listen to and honor your inner voice that says, I'm awesome! That way, no one will be able to rent valuable space in that precious little noggin of yours. You are a holy vessel. Be brave enough to always believe that. It's not arrogant to think your God's greatest gift; it's love, and remember, love is what you're best at.

Your strength is in your ability to be bravely unique. You'll feel that looking like everyone else is boring and has very little divine purpose. Like what in the world are we accomplishing here by trying to look pretty? Aren't there bigger fish to fry? Like who's on second base and how are we going to get the third out?

Your fierce bravery will be a rising tide that lifts all boats. Most of your girlfriends are waiting for you to make the move, to feel good enough just the way you are, so allow them the same feeling by being brave enough to own it. They'll thank you for your courage and permission to be beautiful just the way they are. And they will support you immensely in the years to come. That bravery you own will make you feel full and good and happy. You'll say things like, "I've never felt closer to God. I've never felt closer to myself." Little me, you were born to be brave.

Being an athlete has taught you that your body is a tool to be used for movement that's fun and life giving. Your body is not meant to look a certain way; it's meant to work. To be useful. Being an athlete makes you a leader, and leadership and teamwork will be as important to you as are going to school and learning.

All the leadership training you're getting now by wearing heavy catcher's gear every weekend, shouting directions across the field to your teammates, committing to team goals, attending every practice, calling the signals, and telling your teammates what to do when the ball comes to them, and conflict management with girl drama—all these skills will be absolutely necessary in your life.

One day, you'll have enough courage and leadership skills to believe in yourself. You'll believe you can teach women and men, girls and boys, that they're great just the way they are. You will share your love with them in so many kind, gentle, and generous ways.

You're brave enough now to ask Mom for help whenever you need it. Bullies, diets, body image, questions about your body, questions about boys and friendships—ask Mom. She wants to see you win, not suffer in silence. She wants to elevate your bravery, lift you up. That's her medicine; let her support you with it.

Never feel ashamed to ask her questions. Talking to Mom will always help you, and you'll feel so good you did it. Your thirty-year-old self promises that.

You are a remarkable young woman, Emily. I love your pigtail braids, the dirt smeared across your chin from your catcher's mask, and your fierce bravery going onto the softball field and shouting positive affirmations to your teammates. You'll use all these lessons in the next eighteen years as tools to inspire and motivate others to keep moving forward on their own journeys until they find the light, essentially the love, for everything and everyone including themselves.

You're a complete magic trick. How could your precious, pure spirit be so perfectly tucked into that beautiful, capable earth suit of yours? I love you so much. You're a miracle. How could you not be, Emily? You're a child of God. And you are perfect just the way you are.

I love you forever,


Emily

*Emily Nolan is the author of My Kind of Life.com. She's also a model and the founder of TOPLESS yoga. #TOPLESSbyemily is a bras-on, bellies-out self-confidence event used as a tool to promote self-love. This event is about exposing vulnerabilities by practicing radical self-acceptance.*

*Emily's effort to share what is real and authentic in media was the catalyst for the #HealthyBellySelfie social media project contributing to the global conversation about body image. Emily speaks publicly about her journey through ten years of disordered eating, plastic surgery, body dysmorphic disorder, and shame. She believes that honesty in conversation can spark individual transformation.*

PART FOUR

For the Girls

*Her mother taught her how to breathe fire so that*
*if they ever threw her to the wolves,*
*she could set their hearts aflame.*
—Nikita Gill

**A**fter having done so much work on ourselves, let's harness that power and create the same for our children. While I speak mostly of girls, as I know them best, I encourage mothers of sons, grandmothers, aunts, and anyone else who has little ones, adolescents, or teenagers in their lives to read this section. It will offer great insight into healthy friendships and developing early self-talk and esteem. If you in any way influence a child, this is for you.

I recently hired an executive coach who works specifically with top performers and executives. I expected lots of discourse on sales tactics and time management, so I was stunned when as we discussed the balance between my work and personal life, he announced, "Your relationship with your daughter is your laboratory."

I thought about that statement for several days. Isn't that what life is—an experiment in living, in relating? No one—no psychologist, pundit, or philosopher—has the clear-cut answers to parenting, healthy marriages, or conflict resolution. We use our lore, our experiences, and our internal compasses to develop ourselves and our children. Examining each through a different lens, one of awareness and critical thought, gives us the greatest hope for building thoughtful, well-adjusted little humans.

My daughter has known from the time she was little that she has no boss. No one lords over her. No one tells her what to believe. She is not owned. Her parents are her guides and protectors. We are there to help her learn to think and reason and build her belief system, but we are not the only influencers in her life. When she questions, I ask her, "What does your heart say?"

It is important that we also assist her in building her expectations about healthy relationships, and that starts with those we surround ourselves with and whose conversations she may overhear.

— Chapter 28 —

Your #girltribe

In previous sections, we talked specifically about the relationships we allow in our lives and selecting and at times deselecting friendships. Yes, it's important that we do this for our self-esteem and health, but we don't often think of the effects our relationships have on our children. We are modeling healthy friendships, relationships, and boundaries for our children without being consciously aware of that. How much more impactful it would be for our little ones to see their moms surrounded by strong, confident, loving women as opposed to those who gossip and speak disparagingly of others. A girl cannot be what she cannot see. Moms, all eyes are on you.

One of my closest girlfriends is a trained dancer. Her entire career has been based on her body's performance and presentation. She notices the flaws of her body in ways that make other women ask, "What are you talking about?" I'd gotten used to it over time, so when she'd complain, I'd jump in and say, "Well, I hate my belly" or "I know, I wish my thighs didn't touch." It was a way of relating, making her feel better and letting her know she wasn't alone in her self-hatred. We'd diminish our bodies in solidarity.

Our daughters are only three weeks apart in age, and while we never paid attention to the way we talked about ourselves pre-kids, we realized it once the girls were old enough to start mimicking us. We made a promise to one another—whenever one of us would speak negatively about herself, the other would immediately sling compliments her direction to reset her. "Jennifer, your eyes are beautiful. You're such a great cook. You're so creative." She'd laugh and say, "You're an excellent writer. You have a great smile. You're such a great mom."

One of our other friends, who didn't suffer from our affliction and hadn't been let in on our new game, thought we were nuts, but it was effective. We cut out our negative double-talk on the spot and sat in the warmth of the other's compliments.

Surround yourself with women who want to sit with you in the warmth of your strengths, women who won't allow you to wallow in self-doubt or take delight in your pain. Call each other out on the conversations filled with words that do not move you to the best version of yourself. Pay attention to the feelings you have deep in your chest when you leave a friend. Are you uplifted? Did you inspire one another? Did you support one another? As Jessica Moore would ask, "Are you leaving that person better than you found her?"

If you've decided to remove any women from your life, consciously consider the caliber of woman you would like to join your #girltribe. What women would you like your daughter to emulate as she learns to build interpersonal relationships? One of the barometers for my friendships has been to ask myself, Would I leave my daughter with this friend for a weekend? If something were to happen to me, would I trust this woman to raise my child to be a strong and beautiful member of society? If the answer to either question is no, I take a closer look at that relationship and its influence on my child and me.

## CHAPTER 29

Creating Your Daughter's
#girltribe

A child's first relationship is with her mother, and as she learns to trust and find her way in the world, she is loyal. Her family is where she finds her primary needs fulfilled—food, shelter, and love. They are cave babies surviving through rudimentary, needs-based fulfillment. It is the core of their existence.

Once we nurture them to adolescence, they begin to see their families as less their universes and more their foundations, the places they root from as they handle the rest of their life experiences. They can always go back to family, and they've been provided the core knowledge and confidence they need to then create their expanded universes. They begin looking to their friends to resolve their emotional needs and find acceptance and comfort as they move into adolescence and into their teen years. These are the first steps out of the nest.

Have you talked to your children about their friendships? Guidance counselors report that as girls move into junior high, the majority of the conversations they have are about girl-on-girl hate, and the intervention is wrapped up in what makes a good friend.

My daughter recently experienced her first girl drama. One of her little friends told her that it was not nice for her to be friends with other kids, and she was bossing my daughter around. She tells Olivia that if she doesn't do what she wants her to do, she won't be her friend anymore. My daughter, devastated that someone would retract her friendship, cries and does what the other girl wants; she fights to get back into her good graces.

Her father and I got on the phone together and explained, "Friends don't force you to do things by threatening you with their friendship or anything else. Friends respect you." We dug into specifics about what a good friend is and expectations, toxic relationships, and boundaries. Many would say, "They're just kids. Let them work it out themselves." But I argue that these moments are the building blocks of the relationships they will have for the rest of their lives. Let's prepare them before hormones get involved.

Setting expectations in relationships gives your children the power to design the friendships that best suit them. They will have the opportunity to determine which characteristics are important to them and which are nonstarters. If friends make them feel sad or guilty or question the core tenets of their strengths—"I know I'm funny, smart, and kind"—they will have the words and self-confidence to call the person out or call the relationship off.

Olivia practiced her boundaries in the car with me the other night. School was starting soon, and she would once again be around her jealous little friend. "Mom, if she starts telling me she won't be my friend again or trying to get me to do things, I'm going to tell her, 'My friends don't talk to me like this, so if you want to be my friend, you have to be kind.'"

Olivia feels empowered. She created her own set of words that felt strong. They were her choice, and they allowed her to find her voice in this starter friendship. She is able to diffuse a situation on her terms and recreate it to be a healthy exercise in boundaries and communication. She also knows her mother supports her wholeheartedly.

Our daughters are the most susceptible to bullying and grown-up issues during their teen years. Sex, drugs, employment, college, and a host of other things start to make their way into their conversations. It's also the time that teens don't think they need us as much, that it's fine for them to flex their independence, but I encourage parents to pay attention to how they are triggered as these issues arise. Are they able to see their children as whole persons navigating new experiences and in need of loving and strong guides? Or is their old messaging about right versus wrong and their refusal to see their children, their babies, as anything more beginning to impede their conversations?

As girls begin to actively seek out and be pursued by boys, many parents find themselves uncomfortable with the impending conversations surrounding romantic relationships. Rather than experiencing discomfort in these moments, it is our opportunity to lean in and prepare them for the transition from girl to woman. They are challenging our vision of childlike innocence, and oftentimes, parents choose to look the other way as opposed to stepping into their roles as strong adult influences. Rather than allowing our children to fumble through the automatic responses that have been ingrained through our familial settings, we can guide them so they can be active participants in the selection of healthy relationships. Talk to them about boundaries, worth, the values they should seek out in partners, and those they can bring to the table as well.

**Do the Work**
**Reflection Point**

- How does your daughter relate to her friends?

- What patterns do you see?

- Can your daughter articulate her feelings in a healthy way?

- Does she have any friends who concern you?

- Have you talked to her about values in friendships?

- How do you feel as more-mature topics arise in your home?

Spend time reflecting on your automatic responses when mature topics arise and how they might differ from what guidance your daughter may need from you.

## CHAPTER 30

Our children come into this world with impressionable minds, big hearts, and bodies that have to see them through. We worry about them from the moment they begin to form in our bellies, yet we sometimes get lost in the business of life. We worry over packed lunches, soccer games, and chores, and we lose focus of the influence we wield in each interaction.

Rather than allowing my child to grow up in response to whatever was on my mind that day, whatever chore or obligation we were meeting, I decided to consciously build messaging around three key areas—head, heart, and health.

It's important to me that Olivia consciously feeds her mind (head) with constructive, positive information. She self-regulates when she sees violence. "Mommy, this is a killing game commercial. I don't want that game." We then talk about the shows she watches so she will actively understand what she is being influenced by, which I examine in greater detail below.

We talk about compassion and generosity (heart) and how important it is to be kind to others especially because we have been given so much.

When it comes to health, we speak of strong bodies and fitness and how they fuel long, healthy lives. We don't talk calories or use words such as fat or skinny.

I am raising a lifelong learner, someone who values knowledge and understands she can come to me for guidance as she's developing her views and opinions. She has absolute respect for adults, but she realizes there's a difference between facts and opinions. My father always told me that I was welcome to disagree with him as long as I did so respectfully, and I have created the same expectation for my daughter.

We talk about the fodder we feed our minds, the things that make us feel good, their purpose in our lives, and how we are to use them. I realized this approach was working when I bought her a super, high-end car seat when she was hoping for a booster. She still hadn't hit the weight requirement, and Mom still researches car seats to get the one that has the absolute highest safety reviews and has been rollover tested. If I could get one with a cage and padding, I would.

This also means her seat is enormous. I tried to highlight its amazing features in a sing-song, run-on sentence: "It looks like a rocket ship chair and it has cup holders and purple stripes and that's your favorite color! Don't you love it?" I had to laugh as she very flatly responded, "Mom, I don't like it when people try to convince me to like things. Please just tell me the facts about safety. Why do I have to have this big chair?" I took a step back. I realized that was not sass but critical thinking at its best. I thought ahead to when a handsome boy would try to sell her on himself. I explained weight requirements, safety regulations, and my desire to keep her as safe as possible at all times. Then she was down with her new chair.

We also talk about what shows she watches and the values of the characters in the shows. She is currently enthralled with "Barbie's Life in the Dream House." While the premise of the show itself is harmless, I don't care for the interactions between characters. Best friends are jealous, Ken and Ryan fight over Barbie, and they even host a game show to see which girl knew Barbie the best. The messaging of popularity and infighting I find troubling, but I want to teach Olivia to notice these things as they arise.

I asked her who her favorite characters were and why. We talked about those who weren't very nice and if we'd want to have them as our friends. We talked about Barbie being nice, pretty, and popular but that those weren't accomplishments to strive for in life.

If Olivia is offered such popularity, I want her to know that she must also accept the responsibility attached. She is to treat it as a platform to discourage bullying, enact appropriate boundaries, and teach others how to be better friends and humans. Conversing with her while we watch a show together instills an awareness of the motivations of the characters and conscientious dialogue.

While we discuss how we feed her mind, it's her heart that I want to remain compassionate. My child has everything she could want in life, so before we have holidays or celebrations, we give to another so we can discuss gratitude. We also bring up gratitude in our prayers at night. I don't suggest you start praying if that isn't your thing, but some questions will let you see into the soul of your child, one being, "What were you grateful for today?"

We also ask God for help—She's working on sassing. I have a sugar addiction. And then we make our requests. "What would you like to ask for?" This opens up dialogue and instills a strong sense of self and faith. I want my daughter to feel comfortable framing requests so as she moves through life, she will be comfortable asking for the pay she deserves and the relationships that are right for her.

Rather than discussing that food can make you fat or that thin is revered, we discuss how to keep the bodies that house our impressionable minds and big hearts intact so they can carry us through life in the healthiest way possible. We are to treat our bodies with respect; we understand that we get one set of baby teeth, one set of grown wo-man (long o) teeth as Olivia refers to them, and that how we treat them is how they will respond to us over time.

We discuss the foods that keep us healthy and moving through life, why exercise is valuable, and how exercising keeps our hearts pumping and our bodies strong. We don't talk skinny. We talk strong and capable.

Olivia's stepmom reached out to me recently to share that she was concerned when she overheard Olivia playing with Barbies and saying, "No one cares about your smarts." We immediately got to work to refocus whatever she was hearing and seeing that we weren't in control of. That included hanging motivational signs in her bathroom—"She believed she could, so she did"—and buying her Cat and Jack play clothes with "Girls Can Do Anything" and "Smart, Strong, and Brave" emblazoned on the front.

A few weeks ago, she was singing in the bathtub and suddenly stopped and asked, "Mom, do you know what I say about you? I say that you are smart, that you have strength and a kind heart." Later, when the song "Most Girls" came on the radio, she sang along. "Most girls are strong and brave and beautiful." She suddenly stopped singing and said, "Like us, Mom!"

Score mom(s).

**Do the Work**
**Head, Heart, and Health**

- What messages do you share with your family about head, heart, and health?

- What could you add to your current messaging that would help your family in this area?

- Do you or your family talk about the influences of TV, social media, and what you feed your mind with?

Consider a family or friend charity project that allows you to give back to the community and set the foundation for compassion, generosity, and gratitude.

How are conversations about health, food, and fitness handled? Do you find your children talking about being fat or skinny? Could we reframe the conversation to instead talk about fit and healthy?

Free-write a paragraph to your children about your wishes for them in regard to their minds (heads), hearts, and health.

— CHAPTER 31 —

Time and experience have taught us that we shouldn't be our children's friends. Children need boundaries, parenting. They like to feel cared for and guided. But as your children move toward adolescence and their teen years, we have to create the space to mentor them. According to Merriam Webster's, parenting is the "raising of a child by its parents." I will let the fact that the dictionary referred to your child as an it sit with you for a moment.

The definition of parent is "one that begets or brings forth offspring" or my favorite, "the material or source from which something is derived." Mentor means so much more; Merriam Webster's defines a mentor as "a trusted counselor or guide."

Consciously moving from the dictionary role of parent, the one that simply requires you to produce offspring and keep them alive, to a purposeful way of interacting can be mind-bending at first. It's a clear shift from automatic to cognitive. I have been asked numerous times how I came into my parenting style, and I offer that I had no choice. I was not mothered in the conventional sense. I do not know what it's like to be mothered and did not have an example to draw from as an adult. A friend recently offered, "It must be exhausting to think through everything you do!" I smiled. "Not when the automatic responses and messaging that started to bubble up came in my mother's voice."

I knew deep within that I would be everything my mother was not. The moment my programming began to surface, I went to work to divorce myself of it completely. I reprogrammed myself. My daughter recently asked, "Mommy, how are you such a good mom?" My heart felt as if fireworks had just been lit as I responded, "I always ask myself, 'If I were a little girl, what would I want from my mother right now?' Then I do that."

The principle of being both a parent and a mentor requires deep self-awareness and the reframing of your role to one of guide. The best way to accomplish this is to look at the world through the curious lens of your children, not based on who you were when you were their age. A friend recently shared that her five-year-old daughter was at the stage where she was curious about herself and doing a little self-exploration. Whenever she'd catch her with her hands down her panties, she'd say, "That's dirty! Go wash your hands!" I argued that her daughter was starting to discover how her body functioned and that telling her that her vagina was dirty might create negative messaging about her body. Rather than creating insecurity about her female parts, could she instead have a conversation about what she's doing and redirect any issues she has with cleanliness in a different way? She was exasperated with my line of thinking. "I explored myself when I was her age. I had an abortion when I was nineteen. I don't want her doing what I did." I softly challenged her. "I did my fair share of exploring, and I didn't have an abortion. You've attached something you are ashamed of to something that's incredibly normal. There are articles from child psychologists on it. Don't make her associate her girly parts with dirt."

Learn to stop yourself in your tracks as you bark parent talk at your children. See their painful moments, failures, fears, and outbursts as opportunities to better understand them and what they need from you to guide them. They will have so many challenging moments in their lives; use those they offer you as testing grounds so when you aren't there to lift them up, fix, or ground them, they will have the foundation to get through it with grace and confidence.

This also lends to one of my pet peeves—when an adult feels threatened by the will of a child. The day your child questions you, can you give yourself space to wonder why instead of feeling as if you're being disrespected? Could they be testing the deliciousness of freedom? Moving from warble to full song? Instead of feeling threatened or as if you have to put them in their place and remind them you're on top, could you instead lean into the moment your child is using to learn and instead turn it into respectful conversation?

My father was brilliant at this. I believe it's why it bothers me so much when I see grown-ups flex their authority muscles with kids who just want to learn how to use their voices. My father earned my deep respect with his extremely calm manner and insistence that I could always say what was on my mind as long as I did so with respect. It was disarming and intuitive. Many times when things were hardest in my home and I'd let my frustrations with my mother be heard, my father would grab his keys and say, "Come on, Catfish. Let's go for a ride." They were the best words I ever heard. I knew I would be seen and heard.

We would drive in silence as we made our way out of the city to the Florida countryside. I always broke first, and I sometimes broke down, but in the end, he guided me toward the right answers. And after we'd resolved all the things on my mind and sitting heavily on my chest, we'd share a banana split at Dairy Queen before we headed home.

Becoming your children's trusted guide and advisor does not make you their friend. It makes you their ally and creates a safe place for them to fall, fail, and be seen.

## CHAPTER 32

My biggest hope is that through the course of internal work, we can move our internal dialogue to healthy self-talk and use it as a catalyst for purposeful girl talk with our children. While I respect that boys need the same language and guidance, I concentrate primarily on girls because women remain a minority, are paid less, and will continue to be criticized for their life choices as we move the dialogue around gender equality forward.

It is imperative that this generation of girls be offered better tools so they will be more prepared as they enter the workforce and their relationships. While my daughter is now only six and conversations are timed based on her needs and developmental progress, it is my intention to be a mom who is available to guide her and her friends as they navigate friendships and boys and move deeper into the world around them.

I've remained active in her friendships by getting to know her friends' parents and creating playdates so we become familiar with the dialogue of the day and the attitude of the parents who influence her friends, and ultimately my child through their interactions. She is being mentored in lockstep with my guidance. Setting this foundation of involvement creates an expectation that I'm available to her and her friends. When we sit for dinner, we talk about what is on their minds and carefully guide them and their choices.

Girl Scouts has been an excellent way for my daughter to build healthy girl relationships that are fostered by women who involve curricula developed by psychologists. It has also done wonders for her confidence and self-esteem. A true introvert, I have never seen her hustle like she does when its time to sell cookies.

I also took a great deal from working with Aleena Valdez, the young entrepreneur and philanthropist whose letter to her future self is included in this book. She curated the content for the entire Girls for Progress conference. I was concerned that we wouldn't be able to keep the attention of twelve- to seventeen-year-olds for a full day, but she made it happen, and they remained engaged and motivated. She incorporated something called Two-Minute Tells where she invited girls to stand up before the group and share something important to them or on their minds in two minutes.

They had free reign of the microphone, and when they were offered a safe space to discuss feelings with their peers while guided by women they trusted, the level of intimacy was astounding. We found out about issues with their siblings, their insecurities, and their need to be seen. In one case, a girl who was sexualizing herself to be interesting ended her two minutes in the tone and timbre of a fourteen-year-old who didn't know how to use her voice.

Girl talk is critical in helping our girls grow into confident women who aren't pinned down by the world's shortcomings or expectations.

Mothers have the power to do that by the way they involve themselves in their lives and how they show them the way.

Can you be the mom who has life conversations with them? You may be the only one who can. Can you bring other mothers together to help build a strong #girltribe around your children? To offer space to allow them to share their concerns and work through their issues? What kind of conversations are you having with them? Do you talk to them about gossip? Bullying? Healthy relationships with boys? Healthy relationships with one another? Do you proactively invite them to be guided and mentored by you, or do you parent them Webster-dictionary style?

**Do the Work**
**Date Night**

Make a habit of having date nights with your daughter and her friends. At some point in the evening, create purposeful conversation. Whether through two-minute tells during which each person at the table shares something that's on her mind or through curated dialogue, get them talking. Actively discuss inner strengths, awareness, and their beliefs, interests, and influencers. Look for ways to turn difficult moments into teaching moments, and rather than discourse, look to discussion. Theirs and yours.

**Do the Work**
**For the Girls: Love Letters to My Future Self**

Offer your daughter the opportunity to revel in her accomplishments and imagine the trajectory she is building as she creates her future. Use the prompting questions below to get started, and offer her the space to truly write her life. Allow her a safe space to share with you what she sees for herself. See her. Hear her. Do not judge her. This is a woman who is becoming whether you like her career choice, her friends, or her plans. Use this opportunity to create more dialogue around what she wants in life, and offer her guidance if she is open to it.

- What am I the most proud of?

- What do I know about myself?

- What do I like most about myself?

- What do I want to do in life?

Now close your eyes and imagine your future or higher self. She knows you and what you are capable of, and she sees such promise. You have an entire world ahead of you. She can see you so clearly, into your soul. She loves you unconditionally.

- What does she look like? Use characteristics. Is she strong? Powerful?

- Where is she?

- What is she doing?

- What is she like?

- What does she want you to know?

- What does she say you need to do to bridge the gap between her and where you are sitting today?

- Do you need to hire a tutor?

- Do you need to take a class?

- Do you need to hire a coach?

- Find your voice?

# Part IV Key Takeaways

- Build your #girltribe, and help your daughter do the same.

- Create opportunities to mentor your daughter, and develop the messaging you find most important for her growth.

- Turn your newly acquired positive self-talk into purposeful girl talk.

- Actively move into the role of mentor for your daughter.

- Help your daughter find her own writing exercise and vision for the future.

— CHAPTER 33 —

The Letters
TO MY
Future Self

Before I spoke at Girls for Progress, I made arrangements for fellow speakers to provide love letters to their younger selves. I interviewed them while we were together in Phoenix. Struck by Aleena, I asked her to pen the very first Love Letter to My Future Self, and I interviewed her on camera. She didn't disappoint. She was an introverted twelve-year-old with a desire to make a difference for girls. Her voice is emboldened by passion and backed up by some amazing parents.

*Aleena Valdez*

Hi, Future Me,

At this time, I am, or I guess you are, or actually we are, twelve years old. Though we are twelve, we have accomplished so much so far! We've been on TV twice and been on an online radio show! Most important, we have raised and donated over $1,000 to the Phoenix Children's Hospital to help kids with cancer.

We also set up a girls' empowerment conference. Our first one is happening in a couple of days. I am sure you will remember the dress you wore with your Chuck Taylors. Though we have had good things happen to us, we need to remember a few things that will help us both out in the future.

Number one: football plays a big part in our lives. We've watched football for years, and we've started playing flag football, which was definitely an eye-opener for us. We've actually learned a lot from it. We learned that people make judgments based on appearance. We of course already knew that being called "just a girl" made us very mad, but when playing flag football, it has come up a lot. Every time it comes up, we want to prove them wrong. Let's always prove those people wrong.

We both know what we are capable of, and we have had so much success so far in trusting ourselves and not listening to what others say we can or can't do. We have also learned to stick up for ourselves. This is huge for us and will be great in the future so people don't walk over us. We know that we are a little quiet sometimes, but we have found our voice recently. We know we don't like to be just average, okay, or content. We like to be given a challenge. We like to be more than average or okay! If we continue this, we can definitely accomplish and exceed any of our goals in the future!

Number two: from doing our Aleena's LemonAid Stand, we have learned quite a bit of stuff. We love to help and inspire others. We also know that you are never too young to change the world. We donate the money to the Phoenix Children's Hospital to help kids with cancer. It goes to purchase books and toys to help them take their minds off their current situations. I want us to continue to help others and donate money to charity.

When we have our own retail shop, hopefully by our sixteenth birthday, we will be able to donate even more money and help even more kids. During the LemonAid stand, we learned that we like to inspire kids and girls. We need to show them that they are never too young to change the world. Be a mentor to them like how Amy Jo Martin is for us.

Number three: We know we are shy and like to stay in our comfort zone, but remember that it's okay to step out of our comfort zone. We have done that a lot of times, but it's been worth it. This so far has been in our social lives. We are still getting plain cheeseburgers when we get fast food. Maybe we will work on stepping out of our comfort zone with food someday. Great things have happened when we stepped out of the comfort zone, so please continue to do so.

Something I need us to remember is that we shouldn't let people tell us what we can or can't do because of our gender or race or just because they feel they can. We know what we can do, we know what we have already done, and we know what we will continue to do. We will continue to prove them wrong. If I continue to be me and you continue to be you, we can continue to be we. We are definitely okay with who we are, what we are doing, and where we going.

Aleena ☺

*Aleena Valdez was eleven when she opened her own business called Aleena's LemonAid Stand. She spells LemonAid with an "Aid" because she donates a portion of her money to the Phoenix Children's Hospital to benefit kids with cancer. To date, Aleena has raised and donated more than $2,500.*

*Aleena lives by the phrase "You are never too young to change the world." She is passionate about making a difference in her community and helping other girls out along the way. She is the founder of Girls for*

*Progress, a conference for eleven- to fifteen-year-old girls. The conference brings amazing speakers together to talk about body image, self-confidence, personal brands, and social media. The conference has three main goals: to inspire girls to make a difference in their communities, to be aware of their social surroundings, and to create a community to support them while they are making a change in their communities.*

*Aleena had her first conference when she was twelve; over sixty girls attend it in her hometown, Phoenix, Arizona. Since then, she has held a conference in Austin, Texas, and she has plans to expand to other cities as well.*

*Aleena is committed to changing perceptions of what kids and girls are capable of doing and achieving.*

— Chapter 34 —

I've been asked numerous times why I was the best person to write this book. At first, the question annoyed me because it came from publishers wanting to be pitched. That felt condescending and disingenuous. You can't sell a movement, a passion—something that burns within.

I have often felt I was unqualified to give parenting advice or tell women how to live better lives, but then I remember where I came from. I had no strong female examples or role models. Everything I do as a mother is consciously constructed, meticulously thought out, and based on what I would've wanted for myself if I had had a strong female influence to guide me. Every failing and misstep has taught me about determination and grit and who I am away from the stories I was told late into the night. I had to step through quicksand, grow through muck, and experience a lot of pain so I could consciously make the world a better place for the women and girls who come next. This is my activism, my advocacy, my pure love.

It is not an accident that I've been writing since I was thirteen. It isn't a coincidence that I went from a patriarchal family to a male-dominated career. The universe conspired, and I have a voice I can't quiet. I recently explained to a friend that if I abandoned this book, I would die. Granted, silvery-tonged author-speak, but it has become so much a part of me that I feel as if a piece of my soul would die if I couldn't share these words with you.

These words, these very important words. If you take nothing else away from this book, know this in your bones and let it be what you think about when things are good, when they are bad, or when they are anywhere in between: You are so powerful. You have the answers, the gifts, the strength within you. You just have to find it for yourself. You can read all the self-help books, go to all the therapy, and practice yoga until your Bakasana Crow is bomb, but until you unlock your power, your voice, and your advocacy of self, you will continue to search.

Do not let the past own you any longer. Now is the time to turn to yourself as your healer and guide. The excavation of your stories and messaging will change your life. Forgiveness of self and others will lighten your load. The strategic power in choosing to choose will turn you into a creator. Your decision to harness this new power and make it a source of guidance for the next generation will offer the world such hope.

We need more hope, so seek your power. It's closer than you think.

*I am fearfully and wonderfully made.*
*—Psalm 139:14*

## — CHAPTER 35 —

# The Author's Love Letter
# to her Younger Self

This is my reckoning. The work I had anticipated and dreaded is upon me. With tentative fingers across my keyboard and a thudding feeling in my heart, I share my love letter to my younger self.

This project has been about everyone else's letters. Their journeys. Their growth. I convinced myself that as a trusted guide and coach, I had earned immunity from writing my own missive. Then Amy Jo Martin called me out, demanded mine, and here we are, honest and nauseous.

I gave myself permission to pour my heart into this book as opposed to being a narrator. I gave myself permission to bleed myself onto the page. I pray it has been helpful to even one woman.

This is the part of my life I didn't want to relive even in words. But I also know in my soul that I would have been fraudulent to avoid it when I preached and professed the power of this cathartic process to others every day of my life and in every page of this book. There is no growth without pain, my love.

So now I write.

Dear me,

You will spend most of your life believing you are unlovable. It will take you a very long time to realize that you came into this world perfect. Everything that came next was information. You will see exacting violence, and you will believe things that are not true. You will believe that small means safe. Quiet means comfort. You will lose faith in people only to find it again. And lose it again. Then find it in yourself.

You will raise a daughter who will banish your makings, your beginnings, when she declares her superpower—"I am so lovable." You will know in that moment that you have rewritten what you know about love, family, and yourself. You will end the cycle, my love, and you will think she is your salvation. She isn't. She is unconditional love and the complete restructuring of your understanding of mother/daughter relationships. She will be five when you realize that you are your own salvation.

I know you are scared a lot. You are surrounded by men who rape, sell, and beat women. You see them thrown on the street in front of your house bleeding until the sirens make their way down Richmere Street. They are choked in their front yards. They are barked at. You will never forget the name of the woman whose body was found when you were ten. Kimberly Hanson. She was twenty-three. She flopped like a fish when she was shot in the head. You shouldn't know that, but you do. You shouldn't know that she was dismembered on the carpet scraps that your dad put out by the street on garbage day after your hand-me-down carpet was installed. You shouldn't know that's how they determined she died when you were seven.

You shouldn't know that your mom and dad looked at pictures of all the trafficked women your neighbor beat to try to figure out who she was since she was unidentifiable from frostbite, inevitable after three years in a freezer. The image of her grave chained to a flatbed truck being escorted down your street will never leave you.

You shouldn't know any of these things, but you do. They will stay with you for your life as does the name of the FBI agent who taught you about luminol and forensic science, Detective Lovejoy. You soaked it all in, bare legged in your threadbare Garfield nightgown.

Their names will haunt you, and you will memorialize them through your advocacy. You will help the girls who look like her. You will let them know they are more than where they came from and much more than the words used to describe them by men who needed to keep them small.

You will know this because you are more than where you came from. You will get out, and there will not be a day that this fact doesn't amaze you. You will sit in gratitude, which sometimes disguises itself as unworthiness. You will say, "I shouldn't be here," and wonder how you aren't a crack whore, but you aren't. No, you are to shoulder their stories and leave your words behind to strengthen the women who come next.

Your dad will be your saving grace, your superhero. While he tirelessly tries to make things better, he never becomes bigger than the things that scare you, and you will mourn his eventual fallibility. He can't fix your mom, but he will show you that you are better than the bumps in the night, the gunshots, the sirens. He will be the reason you become the woman you are today. Love him harder.

You don't understand why your mom doesn't love you. You wonder why she never chose you over her demons, her addictions. You will realize much later in life that she was filling voids you are glad you know nothing about. In her rages and her obliteration, she will shield you from the violence that came before you. She will love you to the best of her ability, but it will be a broken, abusive love, nothing more.

You will feel uncomfortable when you see mothers and daughters show affection. It will seem foreign to you until you hold your daughter in your arms, and then, you will never imagine it any other way. You will completely rewrite what you know about moms, and your child will be the love you sought. I can't wait for you to meet her.

I can't wait for you to meet yourself. You are so powerful. You just don't know it yet.

You will do dumb things, but not too dumb.

You will enter relationships that will empty you, violate you, and break you, but you will always walk away. You will learn to take heart in your intuition, your steel, and become a force. All these hurting men will teach you how to create stronger boundaries, an ironclad sense of self. You will become your own best advocate.

You will leave home in your early twenties and move across the country to figure it out in a new place where you can create your own life. It will be a big, beautiful life, and no one will imagine you grew up on Richmere Street. They will simply see your compassion and intelligence.

You will play big. You will find your voice. You will find security. You will become everything you wanted your mom to be—love. You will become the woman you were looking for in those moments you hugged yourself to sleep.

You have bones of steel and the blood of a warrior, and your heart and mind are diamonds. They may need polishing, they may become dirty, but one day, you will realize their strength leaves indelible marks in the glass of others. On that day, you will realize your power. You have words in your veins like lace and cobwebs. They are built on the tears and violence of the women who came before you, and they grieve and heal for the women who come next.

You were put on this earth to share stories, to heal yourself and others. You are here to end cycles and create the new. Fear will come, but I ask you to look it in the eye, plant your steel legs in the earth, let your diamond brilliance shine like a shield … and tell it to go fuck itself.

You have work to do.

Love,


Me

# Acknowledgments

To Olivia, my everything. Thank you for making me a mother and a better woman. You have made my life so much richer, and I will never stop thanking God for bringing us together again.

To Bill Reishtein, my brand manager and the organizer of my words. You saw promise and sought out to find my North Star. I am eternally grateful.

To the women who provided letters, answered surveys, excavated old stories, and built new ones with me. I am inspired by every one of you, and I thank you.

To my #girltribe— Jamie Little, Jessica Moore, Soraya Aguirre, Jennifer Gagliano, Melissa McKinley, Aliya Fowler, Sadaf Baghbani, Caroline Heldman, Jennifer Shydler Wiley, Alexis Michaud and Liberty Leavitt. Thank you for your unwavering belief in me and the cheering section you built be it individually or collectively.

To my Angel, Christina Ambubuyog. Thank you for your guidance and love. I have grown so much just by knowing you.

To Deven Meguiar, Rhena Griffin, and Amber Lock. Thank you for holding me down, cheering me on, reminding me where my roots were, and celebrating how far I've come. You keep it real, keep it on lock, and keep it moving forward. It is amazing to watch.

To Diana Bennett and David Steen. Thank you for your support and love as I have built this project. I am so grateful to feel the warmth of your friendship and your faith in my voice.

To my writer friends who have been such inspiration and support—Marc Graham, Tracy Brogan, Camille Di Maio, Kimberly Derting, Katie Anderson, SarahFrances Hardy, Lisa and Laura Roecker, Tracey Cleantis, and Randy Susan Meyer. I finally did it, y'all. Thank you for your writerly support. I am so grateful to be part of this community.

To Donna Arrogante, Kathleen Paul, and Bethany Taylor. My team. You make me look like a grown-up. Thank you for your vision and Millennial Magic. I adore you.

To JD. Thank you for Mara and all the weird and wonderful conversations. You were unexpected.

To my #businesstribe—Ted Dake and Johanna Blake. Thank you for understanding that we can't always stop doing the things that burn from within. I'm grateful for your love and support, and I thank you.

To Jim, Barbara, and Jennifer. You have been my greatest teachers. I love you, and I'm grateful. Thank you.

To Luis Maceira. Thank you for making lists, answering questions, and seeing me. I love you.

# Recommended Reading

The Whole Brain Child by Daniel J. Siegel, MD and Tina Payne Bryson, PhD.

Parenting from the Inside Out by Daniel J. Siegel, MD and Mary Hartzell, MEd.

Bringing Up Girls by Dr. James Dobson.

Raising Girls by Steve Biddulph.

Girls Will Be Girls by JoAnn Deak, PhD, with Teresa Barker.

What I Told My Daughter: Lessons from Leaders Raising the Next Generation of Empowered Women Edited by Nina Tassler with Cynthia Littleton.

Gender Lens Investing: Uncovering Opportunities for Growth, Returns and Impact by Joseph Quinlan and Jackie VanderBrug.

Gender Intelligence by Barbara Annis and Keith Merron.

Women, Power and Politics by Lori Cox Han and Caroline Heldman.

The Artist's Way by Julia Cameron.

Radical Forgiveness by Colin Tipping.

Forgiveness: 21 Days to Forgive Everyone for Everything by Iyanla VanZant.

Zero Limits: The Secret Hawaiian System for Wealth, Health, Peace and More by Joe Vitale.

The Next Happy by Tracey Cleantis.

An Invitation to Self-Care by Tracey Cleantis

Choose the Life You Want: The Mindful Way to Happiness by Tal Ben-Shahar, PhD.

Choice Theory: A New Psychology of Personal Freedom by William Glasser, MD.

The Desire Map: A Guide to Creating Goals with Soul by Danielle LaPorte.

White Hot Truth by Danielle LaPorte.

From Anger to Intimacy by Dr. Gary Smalley and Ted Cunningham.

Fight Your Way to a Better Marriage by Dr. Greg Smalley.

Change Your Thoughts—Change Your Life by Dr. Wayne Dyer.

Wishes Fulfilled: Mastering the Art of Manifesting by Dr. Wayne Dyer.

Claim Your Power by Mastin Kipp.

The Universe Has Your Back by Gabrielle Bernstein.

The Identity Bond: A Journey to Self Awareness by Dr. Melanie Ross Mills, Ph.D.

The Couple's Bond: A Guidebook to Promote Relationship Bonding Through Self Discovery by Dr. Melanie Ross Mills, Ph.D.

CPSIA information can be obtained
at www.ICGtesting.com
Printed in the USA
LVHW03s0009250918
591277LV00001B/37/P